Jewish Museums of North America

A Guide to Collections, Artifacts, and Memorabilia

Nancy Frazier

John Wiley & Sons, Inc.

New York • Chichester • Brisbane • Toronto • Singapore

This book is dedicated to Jack, David, and especially Leslie, who was a great help.

In recognition of the importance of preserving what has been written, it is a policy of John Wiley & Sons, Inc., to have books of enduring value published in the United States printed on acid-free paper, and we exert our best efforts to that end.

Library of Congress Cataloging-in-Publication Data

Frazier, Nancy.
    Jewish museums of North America : a guide to collections, artifacts, and memorabilia / by Nancy Frazier.
       p.   cm.
    Includes bibliographical references and index.
    ISBN 0-471-54202-4 (pbk.)
    1. Jewish museums—United States—History. 2. Jewish museums—Canada—History. 3. Jews—United States—Intellectual life.
    4. Jews—Canada—Intellectual life. I. Title.
E184.J5F63 1992
970.004'924—dc20   91-44026

Printed in the United States of America

10 9 8 7 6 5 4 3 2 1

Printed and bound by Courier Companies, Inc.

FOREWORD

The concept of a guide to anything assumes a subject sufficiently complex to require guidance. That Jewish museums should have attained this status is as much a cause for celebration as is Nancy Frazier's achievement, represented by this book.

Jewish museums are hardly a new phenomenon, as this book demonstrates. Indeed, they came into being close on the heels of the 19th-century emergence of history and art museums as we now know them. The oldest Judaica collections in this country are now in their second century, and some of them even predate European collections. Their holdings may range widely, including exceptionally high-quality works of fine and decorative arts alongside artifacts whose only interest is some tenuous Jewish connection. Specialized Jewish archives, libraries, historical organizations, and synagogues also hold material of Jewish interest, and when one adds to these a variety of non-Jewish institutions, one understands better the impressive range through which this book takes the interested reader.

The current energy that is so evident throughout the Jewish museum field derives from more than either conventional museum history or the state of the American Jewish community. It reflects a number of complex societal factors, only some of which have their origins within that community.

Thirty years ago, there were already several significant American Jewish museum collections. Yet the institutions in which they existed were fiscally and organizationally fragile, and thus were severely inhibited from presenting the kinds of exhibition and publication programs we now routinely accept as normal for the field. Moreover, the museums themselves were generally marginal to the interests of most Jews as individuals and to the American Jewish community as a collective entity. It was a time when the conventional community art or history museum was seen as the preserve of the privileged classes. In a parallel sense, the Jewish museum could be seen as the preserve of a few eccentrics (not a group of Jewish patricians)—people with deep personal convictions about Jewish history or artifacts from the Jewish past, who exercised those convictions in spite of a disinterested or even hostile climate.

The organized Jewish community had no time for these pursuits; often, even the larger host institutions (e.g., the rabbinical seminaries), within which the museums generally lived, were relatively indifferent to them. Discussions about issues such as "Jewish art" were treated dismissively as being outside the legitimate concerns of most serious art historians and critics, and at best marginal in relation to Jewish scholarship. (The fact that there were a handful of actively publishing Judaica specialists, such as the late Cecil Roth, only accentuated the general impoverishment of the field.) Indeed, interest in what is now called "Jewish studies" in general was, with few exceptions, encouraged only at Jewish scholarly institutions (i.e., those same seminaries which were confounded by their museum holdings).

The collections themselves were staffed and managed by a motly array of caretakers. Included was a sprinkling of significant European-trained art historians, part of the great wave that fled from Hitler in the 1930s. Academic or museum posts were not available to all who sought them, and this, in turn, was both an unforeseen benefit and an obligation for the Jewish community of that day. Often working with minimal institutional and patron support, these scholars nevertheless advanced the field significantly within a small, but important, group of articles and books. Yet, their dual isolation both as immigrants and as traditional academics tended to reinforce the isolation of the Jewish museums that was already in effect due to simple community disinterest.

An interesting exception was the case of The Jewish Museum in New York, which had attempted to confront mainstream contemporary art issues—and not necessarily Jewish ones—by the late 1950s. Operating under the rationale that enables liberal religion to be inclusive about almost all forms of intellectual endeavor—even the avant garde—the museum operated what can only be described as parallel programs for several years. Its seminal exhibitions of that time have become shrouded in myth for their impact on the larger art world, while relatively little impact was felt on the world of Jewish culture. Moreover, none of the other Jewish museums was about to emulate a program pattern validated only within the confines of the New York art world—a milieu that had even less interest in Jewish cultural issues than did most of the Jewish community of that time (late 1950s, early 1960s).

Nevertheless, a strange residual impact was evident in the reality that people had at least heard of the concept of a Jewish museum (albeit The Jewish Museum was the one they meant). Its operation as a significant player within the context of the museum world of the country's cultural hub could only impact positively on validating Jewish museums generically in the long run. And, indeed, that is precisely what has happened, although the factors that led to the situation which this book surveys are far more complex than one series of exhibitions in one New York museum.

The changes in the American Jewish community over the past thirty or so years have been well documented by specialists. Not all of these changes are deemed good, as one sees in the concern about issues such as increasing intermarriage and decreasing Jewish learning. Yet, this same period has seen the flourishing of Jewish studies departments in colleges and universities across the land, so that there are now far more varied options for those who want to engage in serious Jewish academic study. These Jewish studies departments are largely staffed by a new generation of Jewish scholars, most of them American-trained, and many were trained outside the confines of rabbinical seminaries. This oversimplified description does not do adequate justice to the subject, but there is little doubt that historical circumstances of the Holocaust and generational time have conspired to alter the complexion of the field.

In subtle ways, this has impacted on the development of a new nucleus of trained Jewish museum workers as well, coinciding with the need to replace the previous generation of immigrant scholar/ curators. Just as the museum field in general was expanding in the numbers of people within it, so too, Jewish museums were benefiting from the expanded range of skills now available in the field. No longer needing to be apologetic about pursuing a track that is taken as irrelevant, the Jewish museum worker now may move among the museums in that specific field, as well as within the museum field at large. Indeed, there is now a body of expertise in Jewish scholarship as well as in Jewish artifact studies (to be very generic) that makes it possible for people to envision spending their entire careers within the world—a practically unthinkable notion only a few years ago.

This same period has seen the general expansion of museums in America (and indeed around the world). Existing museums have grown larger, while a seemingly endless number of new ones have appeared on an almost daily basis. This is a reflection of a complex series of social and economic factors: increased and different leisure time patterns among large numbers of Americans; population growth, community development; and more varied fiscal support systems, as local and federal governments began to share in costs that had previously been borne almost exclusively by the private sector. The Jewish community has also been affected by the burgeoning interest in museums, and especially in community museums.

Another factor working in combination with these circumstances has been the growing preservationist thrust, which gained special impetus from the American Revolution Bicentennial celebrations. The impact of this thrust on a new self-consciousness about the American past in general has been extraordinary in many ways that have benefited museums. Jewish historical interests, always at the fulcrum of Jewish cultural sensibilities anyway, grew exponentially in this climate. These interests moved beyond the national organization specifically devoted to this effort (the American Jewish Historical Society) and took root in many communities through new historical organizations, museums, and restorations. This, in turn, led to the development of archival and artifact collections that often grew into expansive museum operations.

A contemporaneous phenomenon has been the gradually altered view of American society in general, away from the simplistic myth of the melting pot to a more complex series of notions about a culturally diverse society in which expression of ethnic distinctiveness is no longer viewed apologetically. This has gradually legitimized a wide range of ethnically articulated and sponsored museums—a situation probably still in its early stages of development. A number of significant Jewish museums were already in existence when this new momentum began, thus putting them in a position to benefit from what was becoming a significant aspect of the museum field in general, while also serving as role models for the kind of collecting and exhibition programs to which many of the new museums aspire. This has been especially true of the larger Jewish museums in major cities. A special irony of this widespread concern for ethnic interests is that general history and art museums are now often also presenters of exhibitions of Jewish interest, thus both validating the work of Jewish museums and also inadvertently creating a kind of competitive environment which can make survival even more difficult for the more "sectarian" (i.e., narrowly focused) Jewish museum.

To this mixture of widely differing factors impacting on the Jewish museum fabric in America must be added the more recent emergence of Holocaust museums and memorials. This is not the place to examine and/or explain why the Holocaust only became so obsessive a subject for the American Jewish community almost a generation after it first was so intensely stamped on the world's consciousness. History plays strange tricks with us, just as we play strange tricks with history. In any case, the Holocaust museum/memorial is in the process of joining the typology of Jewish museums in a manner that will probably not be fully understood for another generation.

As with any other discussion of aspects of American Jewish life, one must take into account the State of Israel. The establishment of Israel did not by itself bring into being most of its major museums, but these museums grew and thrived in ways that have had a salutary influence on America's Jewish museums. This is as true of the extraordinary Judaica and archaeological exhibitions of the Israel Museum (Jerusalem) as it is of the moving ways in which Yad Vashem (Israel's Holocaust memorial) addresses the *concept* of a Holocaust memorial and museum. And the widely influential Museum of the Diaspora (Tel Aviv) has further validated new ways of seeing the Jewish past, even while it deftly challenges lines that traditionally divide authentic historical artifacts from reproductions. Most of the significant American Jewish museums have absorbed aspects of these influences, while returning a measure of their own creativity to Israeli sister museums.

The impact of museums is no longer limited to the experience of the museum visit. Museum exhibitions and collections research often represent major directions in the development of scholarship, subsequently published in books and catalogs. This factor has radically altered the field of art book publishing over the past generation. It has changed the field of Jewish book publishing as well. Jewish museums have been the source of a major library of Jewish publications which have added immeasurably to the fields of Jewish scholarship for the specialist as well as for the general reader.

Perhaps the question one dares not ask is the one that may well be uppermost in the minds of those who lead the many museums described here: Can the Jewish community be counted on for the growing levels of support needed to maintain what is now an impressive array of institutions? This support is not just fiscal, although that is clearly an ongoing challenge to all such institutions. Equally critical is the development of audiences to visit and learn from these museums. The underlying educational programs are already in place at many of these museums, again reflecting much of the creative work taking place in most American museums.

This book is a critical part of that process, which explains why one greets it with such excitement. Nancy Frazier herewith performs a service both to the museums themselves and to the audiences for whom they were created.

TOM L. FREUDENHEIM
Assistant Secretary for Museums
Smithsonian Institution

PREFACE

At the Jewish Museum in New York, in the early 1980s, I was troubled by how little I understand about the religion of my ancestors. The spectacularly beautiful objects on display—embroidered Torah curtains, silver basins, portraits—alluded to the continuity of Jewish life and culture over centuries and across continents. But I didn't really know what they meant.

Since I began writing about museums about 10 years ago, I have become thoroughly addicted to the glorious education museum going provides. Objects in museums give form to history: a gold filigree wedding ring from 17th century Venice is a lovely piece of jewelry, but, more significant, it speaks of the settlement and practices of Jews in Italy at the time. Museums collect things. Things represent ideas.

I knew that exploring Jewish collections would be tantamount to exploring Jewish history.

There are about 10 major Jewish collections in North America; another 20 to 30 smaller collections were often developed through the efforts of local congregations or visionaries who understood the teaching power of their treasures. Teaching is a primary impulse behind the ever growing number of Holocaust museums. As the survivors age and pass on, the objects that represent their bravery as well as their suffering serve to illuminate a period of history.

Beyond those obvious kinds of collections, I launched a treasure hunt for more unconventional fragments of Jewish life and settlement in North America. I looked for sites, artifacts, singular images, and exhibits that added pieces to the puzzle that was taking shape. How can I define those pieces I finally chose to include here?

At the annual conference of the Council of American Jewish Museums, one of the speakers told a story that illustrates ethnicity:

It happened that one day Stalin got a letter. He read it with astonishment. Then his surprise turned to pleasure and

finally to victory. The letter said, "I was wrong. You were right.
I should apologize. [signed] Lenin."

A conference of the Central Committee was called to celebrate the turn of events, and high officials from all over the
Soviet Union came to read the letter. There was a great roar of
congratulations and celebration.

Among the participants was a little Jewish man who raised
his voice above the commotion to ask, "May I read it?"

"Of course," he was told.

So he climbed onto the stage and, standing behind the
podium, read aloud:

"I was wrong? *You* were right? *I* should apologize?!"

Many of the places and objects included here are "Jewish" as a
matter of interpretation or inflection. But I believe they are significant parts in the picture puzzle about Jewish life that I have tried to
assemble. If some of my choices seem a bit arbitrary or even eccentric, it is only because they are.

Be assured, however, that all the major Jewish museums of
North America are included here, to the best of my knowledge and
conscientious research. Also included are historical societies that
have Jewish artifacts on exhibit, and libraries that contain extensive
or unusual Judaica, or mount exhibits, or contribute to exhibits of
Jewish content.

Judaica refers to objects that have a distinctly Jewish flavor,
from books to Yiddish New Year cards to Hanukkah lamps, Torah
ornaments, ceremonial cups, and other objects used in religious
ceremonies. Wondering why these items, simple or elaborate, are so
exquisite, I came to appreciate the concept of heightening the sanc-
tity of a mitzvah—a religious duty or a commandment of God—by
embellishing the object used to perform it.

Synagogues that have significant collections of art or Judaica are
included, but, although a number of synagogue buildings are architectural works of art, I have not included them for that reason alone.

Included are a few single works by artists as various as
Rembrandt and Chagall, in which the theme is deeply, movingly
Jewish. I have omitted paintings by Jewish artists that do not have
such specific content.

I have been encouraged by the commitment of three far-flung generalist museums—in Toronto, Raleigh, and New York City—in devoting precious gallery space to Jewish culture. It raises hopes that other large museums might follow suit.

One type of museum I tried to find, but didn't, is a historic house furnished by a Jewish family of a particular period—the early years of the 20th century, for example, when so many Eastern Europeans came to the United States. Such a place would be wonderfully instructive, and perhaps someday a setting like that can be reconstructed.

I have tried to be inclusive rather than exclusive, but if I have missed any significant listing, please let me know.

I must stress the importance of calling ahead if you plan to visit any of the sites described. Museum hours are listed, but they are always subject to change. I have not listed admission fees for that same reason. Some museums do not "charge" an entrance fee, but they expect a contribution. The status of accessibility for handicapped visitors is constantly changing and should be queried in the advance phone call.

This project—this education—about Jewish art, history, tradition, ritual, and culture has been indescribably rewarding. It is my ardent hope that readers will share the enormous pleasure and sense of enrichment this work has given me.

NANCY FRAZIER

Leverett, Maine
December 1991

ACKNOWLEDGMENTS

Elizabeth Knappman made the book come true.

I thank two excellent professors in the Art History Program at the University of Massachusetts, Amherst, who helped me to explore important ideas that inform the text: Mark Roskill and Craig Harbison.

Belden Randolph Merims is a wonderful museum-going companion whose enthusiasm and knowledge were a bonus.

CONTENTS

❧ ❦

NORTHEAST

CONNECTICUT

❧ DOWN WITH HAMAN! ❧

CONGREGATION BETH ISRAEL JUDAICA MUSEUM
701 Farmington Avenue
West Hartford, CT 06119
203-233-8215
Hours: By appointment.

Just outside the doors to Beth Israel's congregational library, objects from the museum collection are presented in a small display case. When I visited, the mini-exhibit included six dried roses and the following story. Rabbi Abraham J. Feldman, who headed the congregation from 1925 to 1968, established a tradition that children being confirmed would carry six roses. After the event, one rose from each child was to be left in the ark, four were to be distributed—to the rabbi, a teacher, a parent, and a service organization—and the sixth was to be pressed.

Rabbi Feldman was a man of power and persuasion. He was the force behind the founding of Beth Israel's museum, located in a room on the second floor. The collection is comfortable, a mix of memorabilia and antiques, and some new objects that fill in gaps. Barbara Richman, who chairs the museum committee, acquired a beautifully colorful, ceramic havdalah set—kiddush cup, candle holder, and spice box, used to usher out the Sabbath with prayer—made in 1987. The museum also owns a more traditional silver set,

1

of older provenance, and the stylistic contrast shows how the same purpose is served by objects that look very different from one another.

In a corner is the Peace Clock, a large grandfather clock made in 1979 to commemorate the signing of an Israeli–Egyptian peace accord concluded the year before. The clock's decorative carvings are symbolic—wheat sheaves representing peace, for example—and Hebrew homilies mark various hours. At 1:00: "The time is short and much work is to be done." At 7:00: "It is always better to get a head start." At 11:00: "The day is still long and there is time to act." On the half-hour and the hour, the clock plays a well-known tune: "Hevenu Shalom Aleichem."

My favorite piece is a Purim grogger (noisemaker). During the late winter festival of Purim, decorum is replaced by a carnival atmosphere. Feasts and masquerades celebrate Queen Esther's success in saving the Jews from annihilation. The wicked Haman, an advisor to Esther's husband, King Ahasuerus, had persuaded the king that the Jews were scheming to overthrow the monarch. Esther was able to prove to Ahasuerus that Haman himself was plotting the king's demise.

The scroll of Esther, the Megillah, which tells the story of Purim, is read aloud during the festival ceremonies. Whenever Haman's name is spoken in the reading, a commotion is raised as if to obliterate any mention of the wicked plotter. Groggers, which resemble New Year's Eve party noisemakers, serve to drown out Haman's name.

The silver and brass grogger in this collection was made in Poland during the 1920s. It represents a Cossack pilloried before a post. His hands and neck stick out of a board, or stock, that is engraved with Hebrew lettering. He has a horrified expression on his face. At the waist, he is chained to the post. His legs are bowed and his boots rest on the top of the handle of the grogger. When it is twirled, a metal arm attached to the tree scrapes against the serrated metal below the Cossack's waist.

DELAWARE

❧ REBECCA ❧

DELAWARE ART MUSEUM
2301 Kentmere Parkway
Wilmington, DE 19806
302-571-9590
Hours: Tuesday, 10 to 9; Wednesday through Saturday, 10 to 5;
Sunday, noon to 5.

Rebecca Gratz is more than beautiful, Sir—she is irresistibly charming. There is an expression about the eyes unlike anything else I have ever seen—an intimation of a depth and an understanding beyond the ordinary. And those eyes themselves are like black, lustrous pools, reflecting centuries of tragic history. I wish you might look into them, as I have, and find yourself curiously moved. She is like a heroine of the Old Testament, wearing the clothes and using the speech of our own day, yet seeming to revert constantly to the past. I am devoted to her as to one who shares my deepest sorrows with rare understanding.

This profession of admiration for Rebecca Gratz was spoken by Washington Irving during a visit to Sir Walter Scott. Sir Walter was duly impressed.

Sometime later, in a letter to Irving, Scott asked: "How do you like your Rebecca? Does the Rebecca I have pictured here compare well with the pattern given?" The letter accompanied Scott's new novel, *Ivanhoe*, in which Rebecca Gratz served as a model for the heroine.

Washington Irving also introduced Thomas Sully, one of America's most skillful and famous 19th-century portraitists, to Rebecca. She was 26 at the time of the introduction, but Sully did not paint her until she was in her 50s. In the portraits, she looks not a day over 27. Perhaps revealing his own fantasies, Sully described Rebecca's beauty as "all that a princess of blood Royal might have coveted."

Rebecca Gratz is usually identified as a prominent Philadelphia educator. In 1838, she established the Hebrew Sunday School Society, and she was one of the founders of the Female Hebrew Benevolent Society.

She never married, but not for lack of suitors. Samuel Ewing, a handsome young man who courted her, extolled her charm in print, saying that all the poets of the past who wrote of the fairest ladies were only prophets of her beauty, of which there were no poets skillful enough to sing.

Of the three portraits Sully did of Rebecca, the one at the Delaware Art Museum was the second. Another is at the Rosenbach Museum & Library (in Philadelphia; see page 107). Commissioned by her brother, Hyman, the painting shows Rebecca's face in profile. Her back is to the viewer and her far shoulder seems to be uncovered. A few soft curls have emerged from under a large, flat, turbanlike hat. The story is that the family rejected this portrait because of the unconventional hat, but one might also hazard a guess that the curls, the pose, and the wistful look might have made the portrait a trifle too sensuous for a proper Philadelphia family. There is a powerful resemblance between this image and one of the most outright romantic idylls of the time. In about 1825 or 1827, the great Goya, then in his 80s, idealized youth and beauty in his last great work, a painting called *The Bordeaux Milkmaid*. He died in 1828. The portrait of Rebecca in the Delaware collection is practically a mirror image of Goya's milkmaid.

DISTRICT OF COLUMBIA

🍃 A LETTER FROM GEORGE 🍃

THE B'NAI B'RITH KLUTZNICK MUSEUM
1640 Rhode Island Avenue, NW
Washington, DC 20036
202-857-6583
Hours: Sunday through Friday, 10 to 5.

One of the prizes of this museum is a small mantel clock. The most famous clock with Hebrew letters on its face is on the tower of Jewish Town Hall in Prague, Czechoslovakia. The Klutznick clock has the same outspoken spirit and, although microcosmic relative to the Prague landmark, it is far more elaborate.

No more than six inches high, the Klutznick clock is made of brass and thought to be from late 19th-century Vienna. The hands are in the center of a painted Star of David. The pendulum swings over a silver-plated Decalogue that is held and guarded by two lions. Columns on either side are wound with silver vines. The Hebrew inscription on the base reads (with a misspelling) "Take us back, O Eternal, to Yourself, And we will come back; Renew our days of old." The words are from Lamentations 5:21—a plaintive verse in a chapter that asks "Why have you forgotten us utterly, Forsaken us for all time?"

This extravagant little clock fits nicely into a diverse collection that includes a very beautiful Russian mizrach, made in 1810—a gift to a friend, according to its Hebrew lettering. It is one of the most delicate, charming papercuts to be found. The theme is a little difficult to distinguish, though a Hanukkah lamp with a woven base is clearly the central focus, and the two guardian lions flanking the lamp certainly fit into the Judaic tradition. Beyond those figures, the symbolism is fanciful. The shape can be described as that of a circus wagon, and it is surrounded by birds, squirrels in cages, fish, flowers in urns, nuts, vines, and trees that spread extravagantly sinuous branches. The colors are soft greens, blues, and beige.

These treasures are in its permanent collection, but the museum hosts many important traveling exhibitions. Several years ago, I saw there an exceptional show on the Jews of China. The Klutznick collaborates with other museums such as the Smithsonian Institution to benefit the public with major exhibitions, for example, Jewish Life in Terezin and Treasures from the Czechoslovak State Collections. As a project of B'nai B'rith, the museum is part of the largest and oldest Jewish service organization in the world.

The museum was opened in 1957 and continues to grow in size and scope. Today, the collection spans the Jewish experience worldwide. Ceremonial and folk art from the permanent collection, much of it donated by Joseph and Olyn Horwitz, is on display in the Cycle of Life gallery.

In 1948, Joseph Horwitz was in Europe on a mission of helping Jewish war refugees to resettle in Israel. Despite his protests, the father of one of the last families he helped pressed a package into his hands. Inside was an exquisite silver Hanukkah menorah from the 18th century. Horwitz and his wife soon decided to make sure that as many as possible of such objects "of simple beauty and reverence from the still warm ashes of the Holocaust" were saved. They became collectors and benefactors of the museum.

One of the Horwitzes' gifts to the museum is an early 18th-century baby's bonnet believed to be from either Italy or France. It is made of white silk trimmed with lace and embroidered with silk thread, metallic lace, sequins, and ribbons. It looks very unbabylike. European christening customs influenced the making of articles of this type and other fancy clothing for Jewish babies. This bonnet, worn by an eight-day-old Jewish boy, may have matched an equally elaborate embroidered tunic made for the child's circumcision ceremony. The bonnet reflects the era in which it was made as well as the opulence of the family for whom it was created.

One of the important documents of early Jewish life in America is George Washington's letter to the Hebrew Congregation of Newport. A facsimile of the letter hangs on the wall of Rhode Island's Touro synagogue; the original is here. In this letter, Washington uses the ringing phrase "to bigotry, no sanction, to persecution, no assistance." The words had already been formulated by Moses Seixas, who had used them in welcoming Washington to Newport.

Whoever said it first, the phrase was worth saying and deserved to be repeated as often as possible.

The B'nai B'rith International headquarters, which houses the museum, is also the location of a sculpture garden featuring bronze works by Phillip Rattner—*Jacob and The Angel*, *Priestly Blessing* (hands rising from a Torah scroll), and *Gabriel* are among them. Rattner's figures often have lumpy, highly polished surfaces or, as in the garden, matte finishes but exaggerated curves. An S is formed by the angel in Jacob's arms and another by the voluminous sleeves of Gabriel.

Highlight: *The B'nai B'rith Klutznick Museum's new Sports Hall of Fame recognizes Jewish sports heros like sportscaster Mel Allen, Boston Celtics basketball coach and mentor Arnold "Red" Auerbach, pitcher Sandy Koufax, quarterback Sid Luckman, journalist Shirley Povich, and Olympic multimedalist Mark Spitz.*

≈ PATRIOTISM ≈

**JEWISH WAR VETERANS NATIONAL MEMORIAL
MUSEUM, ARCHIVES AND LIBRARY
1811 R Street, NW
Washington, DC 20009
202-265-6280
Hours: Monday through Friday, 9:30 to 4:30.**

To preserve a record of the patriotic contributions of the men and women of the Jewish faith who served during and between times of war in the Armed Forces of the United States and as veterans thereof, from the time of the founding of this country to the present, for future generations by illustration through public education utilizing the Museum's collections for exhibits, publications, and educational programs.

That clear, if dry, statement describes the purpose of this museum, which houses a powerfully moving collection. The patriotism of American Jews is often a deep and passionate devotion. Since the country's beginning, the promise of freedom in America has meant life itself to Jewish immigrants, and they and their descendants have served unfailingly and with conviction in the U.S. armed forces. As a personal and public expression of pride in citizenship and gratitude to the freedom granted by the United States, many Jews have given their lives.

The right to serve was a privilege that, in the past, had to be fought for. Asser Levy, a kosher butcher, was among the first immigrants. He came from the Netherlands and landed on today's Manhattan Island in about 1654. New Amsterdam's Governor, Peter Stuyvesant, tried to prevent Jews from serving in the militia by levying a tax on them and declaring they should "remain exempt from general training and guard duty." Levy and a Jewish colleague demanded and won the right to stand guard at the stockade. After several unsuccessful efforts, Levy also was allowed to become a citizen. He was the first American Jewish veteran.

Joseph Ira Goldstein was born in Roosevelt, New Jersey, in 1942. He graduated from Rutgers University in 1964, went on to Officers' Training School, and became a Naval Flight Officer. In Vietnam, he flew about 110 missions and received the Navy Unit Commendation Medal, the Vietnam Gallantry Cross, five air medals, and other commendations and awards. His heroism, patriotism, and Judaism go hand-in-hand.

These two veterans, centuries apart, are but two of the people whose service to the country is documented at this museum. Beyond the coach light by the door and elegant fanlight above the entrance, the red brick building offers discoveries of many kinds. Information provided in both the archives and the exhibits greatly enhances our historical knowledge of the Jewish presence in America. Visitors learn, for example, that President Abraham Lincoln is generally thought to have been a great supporter of the Jews. Lincoln had rabbis serving as military chaplains, sent a Jew, Dr. Isachar Zacharie, as his peace emissary to the South, countermanded General Ulysses S. Grant's order prohibiting Jewish merchants from doing business with the Army, and referred to a Jewish lawyer from Quincy, Illinois, as "my closest friend."

The artifacts on view include uniforms (World War II WAC and Red Cross issue, and a wool overcoat worn by a World War I doughboy, for instance), arms, flags, maps, and wonderful old photographs. One group of photos, dated 1912, shows 51 portraits of members of the Hebrew Union Veteran Association, "Survivors of the War for the Maintenance of the Union of the United States of America 1861–1865." There could hardly be a more diverse looking group, though they all sport mustaches and wear their medals with panache.

From World War I come bugles, binoculars, stirrups, a brass whistle on a chain, and a small advertising card displaying the Star of David and inviting "Soldiers-Sailors-Marines! For You when in New York, Good Eats—Fine Sleep & Loads of Fun at New York City Branch, Jewish Welfare Board."

The posters are accurate popular reflections of their times. One, printed during the 1930s, shows the Star of David with an American eagle in the center (the emblem of Jewish War Veterans of the U.S.A.) and carries the impassioned legend: "For Humanity's Sake! BOYCOTT German Industry—DON'T BUY German Goods."

This museum was chartered by an act of Congress in 1958, to commemorate the Jewish Americans who served in the U.S. armed forces in times of war. The museum made several false starts; not until 1990 was a full, energetic staff employed and the present momentum and direction firmly established. The staff actively collects and maintains materials related to the museum's purpose, plans, and exhibitions, and promotes the institution as a viable educational and learning center for scholarly research and development. This is not, however, a military museum in the traditional sense; it is not devoted to the triumphs or glorification of war, or even to the meaning or technology or suffering of war. Instead, this museum celebrates the commitment of Jews to their country.

The collection is evocative, especially for those who can relate to memorabilia of World War II: the battered metal canteen and cooking utensils; the beautiful, sophisticated woman with a pompadour, featured as *Newsweek's* "weekly Pin-up . . . Special for the Armed Forces"; the tattered *Soldier's Guide to Naples*; the "Spotter Cards" for identifying the silhouettes of aircraft; the U.S. Navy sewing kit; poker chips; letters written with a fountain pen on lined paper; a linen towel with a red stripe down the center and the word "Medical" woven into it.

Highlight: *Among the most evocative displays is one that may not make itself clear at a first, hasty glance. What could be so unusual about a small altar with candles, a prayer book, and a small ark? A*

Portable ark and altar. The altar was assembled from objects of war found on the battlefield and transformed into objects of peace. Collection Martin Weitz. Courtesy of Jewish War Veterans' National Memorial Museum, Washington, DC.

more careful look reveals that these objects are resting on a trunk. The portable ark and altar gain more significance when details of their story are filled in by World War II Chaplain Martin Weitz, who conducted services for Jewish troops all over the South Pacific. Dr. Weitz explains the exhibit this way:

Several people helped me assemble objects of war found on the battlefield so that they could be translated into subjects of peace. Among them were the following items: the lid of the trunk has two 37-mm capshells, one of U.S. origin, the other Japanese. Both were suspended from the corners of the lid, and were sounded to announce the beginning of the service. The back of the lid is covered by a silk parachute that floated down with a soldier from a Japanese plane. In the center of the lid we see the Ten Commandments, carved from an aluminum remnant from a Japanese zero plane.

The base of each candlestick is set into a brass ring taken from a 107-mm shell; one ring is Japanese, one American. Underneath the altar surface is storage space for prayer shawls, prayer books, candles, wine, etc.

❦ A CENTER AMONG CENTERS ❧

LIBRARY OF CONGRESS
Hebraic Section
African and Middle Eastern Division
Washington, DC 20540
202-287-5422
Hours: Monday through Friday, 8:30 to 5.

The Hebraic Section is located on the first floor of the Adams Building, in Room LA 1006.

As is true of the Library of Congress collection in general, the holdings in Jewish and Hebraic materials are vast, nearly beyond comprehension. There is no single catalog that lists all the varied Hebraic holdings; a series of catalogs must be consulted.

During the early development of the country, Hebrew was an important part of American intellectual life, a necessary scholarly tool for studying the Bible. As time and archaeological research progressed, Hebrew was important for interpreting new discoveries in the Holy Land.

The Library of Congress had a modest collection until Jacob H. Schiff presented it with gifts of close to 15,000 volumes. Schiff's generosity launched the Hebraic section, and the collection grew and multiplied; almost 125,000 items are now available in the stacks for examination by researchers and scholars. Monographs, periodicals, newspapers, and documentation of Jewish life in Eastern Europe before World War II are in constant demand. Some eccentric and specialized items include the following:

- A Hebrew translation of the Koran;
- An early Ethiopian psalter in Ge'ez;
- Particularly strong holdings in the areas of Bible study and rabbinics, liturgy, Hebrew language and literature responsa, and Jewish history;
- Extensive collections of printed editions of Passover Haggadot;
- More than 1,000 original Yiddish plays, in manuscript or typescript form, written between the end of the 19th and middle of the 20th centuries and submitted for copyright registration to the Library of Congress; they were intended for the American Yiddish Theater;
- Hebrew incunabula—books printed before the year 1501;
- 65,000 books, journals, and other publications from Israel;
- A selection of ketubot.

The list could go on. But other divisions of the Library of Congress clamor for equal attention to their items of Hebraic origin—European, Hispanic, Geographic, Manuscripts, Maps, Music, Photographs, Prints. A full tour is not a one-day amble, because this is one of the *world's* foremost centers for the study of Hebrew and Yiddish materials.

The Photographs division offers unique delights. An extraordinary photograph of Rabbi S. Cohen was taken in 1944 at the Manischewitz Winery in Brooklyn. As seen by a camera far above him, the rabbi appears as a small figure in a white prayer shawl, standing alongside gargantuan wine barrels. He is inspecting Passover wine. A three-quarter-face print of Emma Lazarus has a moiré effect and shows a fine, sensitive face, both intense and gentle. How many days would be needed to do justice to the Broadcasting, Law, Motion Pictures, Rare Books, and Special Collections divisions?

In June 1991, From the Ends of the Earth, a major exhibit of Hebraic and Judaic materials in the Library of Congress, opened in the Madison Building. It is anticipated that the exhibit will travel after it closes, but no schedule is currently available. The Hebraic Section does not display any exhibits, but it frequently contributes materials to Library of Congress exhibits elsewhere.

Highlight: *The Ruth Rubin Collection of field recordings of Jewish folklore is maintained in the Archive of Folk Song. From the late 1940s through the 1960s, Ruth Rubin recorded songs of eastern European origin throughout Jewish communities in Canada, the eastern United States, the United Kingdom, and Israel. She also documented some Yiddish art songs, songs about the lives of immigrants, and songs created by Soviet Jews in the 1920s and 1930s. She is the author of* Voices of a People: The Story of Yiddish Folksong. *The Library of Congress has 126 of her tapes.*

⮜ TO EDUCATE THE LIVING ⮥

THE UNITED STATES HOLOCAUST MEMORIAL MUSEUM
The National Mall
Washington, DC
c/o U. S. Holocaust Memorial Council
200 L Street NW, Suite 588
Washington, DC 20036
202-653-9220
Hours: Opening date (1992) to be announced.

As distance from the Nazi persecution of Jews, Gypsies, Poles, the handicapped and infirm, homosexuals, Jehovah's Witnesses, political and religious dissidents, and Soviet POWs increases, and as those who lived through the Holocaust and bore witness to it grow old and pass away, there is a fear that the evil of that era will be minimized or forgotten. Throughout the United States, Holocaust associations have taken action to make sure that the years between 1933 and 1945 do not slip into oblivion. They reflect the optimistic side in human nature, a belief that by reminding us of the evil we are capable of, we will never be so wicked again.

A Holocaust museum is a difficult idea, philosophically, psychologically, and aesthetically. The questions raised really don't have answers; how can the indescribable be described? How can the events be forsworn so that history won't repeat itself? How does each visitor answer the most provocative question: To what extent is institutionalization of the massacre a means of avoidance—that is, do we use the official commemoration as a way to absolve ourselves of deeper and continuing responsibilities in the face of prejudice, discrimination, and persecution?

Whenever a Holocaust museum or memorial is proposed, these questions are—or should be—raised. The most important achievement of any museum, and certainly any of this genre, is to make us think.

The Holocaust Memorial Museum nearing completion in the nation's capital will be in a building that has won the admiration of one of the country's premier architectural critics, Paul Goldberger of *The New York Times*. He stated the designer's problem succinctly:

If the Holocaust Museum is too beautiful, it risks making this museum too much like other civic buildings, and thereby trivializing the Holocaust by seducing us into believing that it was simply another Big Event in the great sweep of history. If the museum design takes the opposite tack, avoiding the usual grandiose classicism of Washington in favor of an industrial tone that would attempt to evoke the factory-like appearance of the Nazi concentration camps themselves, it could become somewhat kitsch and thus trivialize the events of the Holocaust still more. And if the museum becomes too literal in its presentation of the Holocaust, it will be repellent to visitors and will therefore fail at what may be the one part of its stated task more urgent than honoring the memory of the dead, which is educating the living.

The museum building, which occupies a site adjacent to the Mall, within view of the Washington Monument and the Jefferson Memorial, meets the criteria Goldberger set. It is, he concludes, "superb, thoughtful and perhaps brilliant."

A 1992 opening is scheduled. The museum will serve as the nation's most important educational institution dedicated to teaching about one of the most heinous chapters in the history of the world.

☙ A LOVABLE BUILDING ❧

THE LILLIAN AND ALBERT SMALL JEWISH MUSEUM
Third and G Streets, NW
Washington, DC 20001
202-789-0900
Hours: Sunday through Thursday, 11 to 3; Friday,
by appointment; closed during August.

Notice first the fence around the building. In alternate sections, the straight, wrought-iron pickets curve to form a menorah, and in the center of the entry gate is a six-pointed star. The brick building is narrow and tall; its scale is just a bit strange, which makes it all the more interesting. The windows are decoratively arched. Those on the first floor are standard size, but the upper windows are tall enough to serve two stories.

This is Washington's oldest synagogue building, the original home of Adas Israel Congregation. The congregation was founded in 1869 by 35 German immigrant families who broke away from the Washington Hebrew Congregation when it introduced Reform innovations. The building was dedicated in 1876 with President Ulysses S. Grant in attendance. Despite his Civil War aberration, endeavoring to prevent Jews from doing business with Union forces, Grant was a close friend to some Jewish leaders in the world of high finance.

In 1907, the congregation moved and the building was rented first to the Greek Orthodox Church, then to an evangelical Church of God. By 1946, the first floor had been converted into shops, including a grocery with a big neon sign recommending its barbecued pig! The second story, where the synagogue proper had been, was used as a storeroom.

Saved from demolition in 1966 by its nomination as a National Capital Landmark, the building was acquired by The Jewish Historical

Society of Greater Washington and moved to its present site. With a gift from Lillian and Albert Small, and inspired research, restoration began.

Evelyn Levow Greenberg, whose efforts were key in the project, described some of the process:

> The mikva, a brick zinc-lined ritual pool, was discovered under the flooring of one of the shops in the northeast corner of the building. Finding it explained why the windows of that part of the lower floor were not aligned with those above. They had been moved to give greater privacy to this area, which had its own entry and anteroom. The mikva was identified in 1960 by Mrs. Pearl Kipnis, 92, the last surviving person known to have used it, in 1911.

In 1975, the Adas Israel synagogue building was opened as a museum. The exhibits it mounts are concerned with aspects of Washington Jewish life and history. Open for Business, for example, was an exhibit offering "a nostalgic look at Jewish-owned businesses in Silver Spring, Maryland, 1926–1964." Featured were the personal stories of penniless immigrants who made their way in an area that was once referred to as "the most lonesome spot between Glenmont and the city of Washington."

A recent exhibition, Jewish Athletes in Washington, DC, offered interesting anecdotes.

> Take Sidney Kolker, for example, still considered one of the best linemen George Washington University ever had. His early interest in football apparently confounded his mother, who never grew to fully appreciate the game. "Sidney," she once told him, "Don't be a fool. If they're chasing you, and you have the ball, just give them the ball!"

Highlight: Architectural critic Wolf von Eckhardt called the Adas Israel building "a dear and most lovable little building of utmost simplicity . . . all the more remarkable if you consider that the synagogue was built at a time when many Jewish congregations began building elaborate temples adorned with Romanesque or Byzantine domes. . . ." As you walk around the building, note a cylindrical bay on the east end—opposite the entrance. The bay was built to hold the Torah ark.

Now restored, the bay is also one of the outstanding features on the inside of the building. The design combines Federal and Victorian details—a classical pediment and Victorian side braces—in a way found only in the District of Columbia area, according to Evelyn Greenberg.

◄ MODERN ART ►

HIRSHHORN MUSEUM AND SCULPTURE GARDEN
Independence Avenue at Eighth Street, SW
Washington, DC 20560
202-357-3091
Hours: Daily, 10 to 5.

The Hirshhorn is the Smithsonian Institution's museum of modern and contemporary art. The focus of the collection is on work of internationally significant artists active in the post–World War II era. Many Jewish artists' works are included in the collection, and some of those exhibited have a specifically Jewish theme.

The collection records are not cross-indexed by subject matter, but the curator of paintings quickly referred me to two works by Jewish artists and representing Jewish themes. One is a watercolor by Raphael Soyer, *In a Jewish Cafe*. Raphael and his twin brother, Moses, both notable artists, were born in Russia in 1919. Both were realists who had a humane, liberal outlook. A sensitive perspective is clear in Raphael's watercolor, painted in 1925. The subject of *In a Jewish Cafe* is a man whose head is large in relation to his body, seeming to reflect the burdens he has on his mind. With his hat on, he looks up from his newspaper. From the distant, tired expression in his eyes, one can almost feel the sadness in his heart.

The second artist, Philip Guston, was born in Montreal in 1913. He moved with his Russian émigré family to Los Angeles in 1919. In addition to an earlier, abstract work of Guston's, the Hirshhorn owns *Ancient Wall*, done in 1976. Though not abstract in the conventional sense, this is an assemblage of forms set against a brick wall. According to the museum's write-up, the forms represent the soles of shoes and limbs, though the limbs are not realistically defined. *Ancient Wall* is a strange, unsettling picture.

❧ SYNAGOGUE CARPET ❧

THE TEXTILE MUSEUM
2320 S Street, NW
Washington, DC 20008
202-667-0441
Hours: Monday through Saturday, 10 to 5; Sunday, 1 to 5.

The Textile Museum has the largest and most important group of Mamluk carpets in the world. Mamluk carpets were produced during the rule of the Mamluk sultans in Egypt. The quality of the materials, richness of color (achieved by using a dye made from an insect residue called *lac*), and extremely high level of technical competence set these carpets above most others.

One Mamluk dates later than the majority, which were produced during the 13th to 16th centuries. This 17th-century carpet has a Hebrew inscription from Psalm 118: "This is the Gate to the Lord through which the righteous shall enter." Whereas the earlier Mamluks were generally geometric in pattern, the synagogue carpet has an elegantly flowered border surrounding two pairs of columns with an arch above them—"the Gate to the Lord." Against a deep red background is a tree-like menorah shape from which hang what look like nine Ner Tamids (eternal lights). The Mamluk is called a synagogue carpet because it is believed to have been used as a curtain for a Torah ark. It is one of only two such antique synagogue carpets known in the world, and it is extraordinarily beautiful.

Because of the fragile nature of fabric, no single object in the museum is left exposed to the light for a long period of time. If you want to see this synagogue carpet (or another, less well known, from Turkey), it is absolutely necessary to call ahead and see whether arrangements can be made to look at these treasures.

◆ WILSON ◆

THE WOODROW WILSON HOUSE
2340 S Street, NW
Washington, DC 20008
203-387-4062
Hours: Tuesday through Saturday, 10 to 4.

The twenty-eighth president of the United States, Woodrow Wilson, was inaugurated in 1913. He was the first American president to nominate a Jew, Louis Brandeis, to the Supreme Court. Brandeis was one of Wilson's three closest advisors.

Upstairs in Wilson's bedroom, standing on the floor next to the mantel, is a bronze statue, about two feet high, that the President was very fond of. Its full name is *The Exiled Son of David*, but it is better known as *The Exile*. Dated 1911, the statue is of a man carrying what is believed to be a small child on his right arm. The base carries an inscription, in Hebrew, from Lamentations: "Her children have gone into captivity before the enemy." The sculptor, Jules Leon Butensky, was born in Russia but lived in the United States from 1904 until his death in 1947.

According to a thank-you note President Wilson sent to Isaac Goldberg in September 1913, the sculpture is a "replica." By using the word replica, Wilson was probably referring to the casting process rather than suggesting that the bronze is a copy.

Information about this piece at the Wilson House is sketchy. Because Louis Brandeis was a supporter of Zionism, however, it is plausible that the sculpture is a reference to that movement.

MARYLAND

❧ MEZUZOT ❧

CHIZUK AMUNO CONGREGATION
8100 Stevenson Road
Baltimore, MD 21208
301-486-6400
Hours: By appointment.

Dissidents from the Lloyd Street synagogue (see the next entry) formed Congregation Chizuk Amuno in 1871. The Congregation is now in its fourth synagogue building, a splendid contemporary complex of which the main sanctuary was dedicated in 1962. Its curving roofline imitates the rolling Maryland countryside, and the stone walls at the entrance reach out as if in welcome.

The mezuzah on the central entrance door was used on the entrance to the Palestine Pavilion at the 1939 World's Fair in New York City. It is one of many more you discover in the museum.

Mezuzah is actually the Hebrew word for doorpost, but it has come to mean the small objects beside the doorway of Jewish homes. The tradition of placing a mezuzah on the right side of every door is derived from the Book of Deuteronomy, where Jews are commanded to place the Law of God on their doorposts. The small containers hold scrolls with selected verses from the Torah.

Containers for mezuzot (plural) are made in many shapes, from wooden fish to the more familiar cylindrical capsules. Dozens of mezuzot are in one display case here.

In another case are objects representing the Jewish home. These include candleholders, cups, a platter, linen, prayer books, and spice containers. There is a colorful Polish papercut mizrach and a case of clay bowls and pitchers to show the utensils used by Jews in the ancient world.

Highlight: *Among the most important treasures is a pair of 18th-century silver rimmonim, or finials, the decorative tops for the poles around which the synagogue scroll is wound. These are Venetian and have few equals for elaborate silverwork.*

❧ IN OLD BALTIMORE ❧

THE JEWISH HISTORICAL SOCIETY OF MARYLAND
15 Lloyd Street
Baltimore, MD 21202
303-732-6400
Hours: Tuesday, Wednesday, Thursday, and Sunday, 12 to 4; other
times by appointment; library and archive, Monday through Friday,
9:30 to 4, by appointment.

*All Baltimore should be grateful to the Jewish Historical Society
of Maryland for creating this one-room exhibition hall discreetly link-
ing the beautiful Lloyd Street Synagogue and still-functioning and
beautiful B'nai Israel Congregation as part of a larger, outdoor Jewish museum where the immigrant population first settled after leaving
the docks.*

So proclaimed an editorial in *The Sun*, a Baltimore newspaper, on
November 27, 1987.

The unique three-building complex so enthusiastically supported is in a section of the city called alternately Old Baltimore,
East Baltimore, and Inner Harbor. It was once a bustling Jewish
neighborhood, but only a few of the businesses run by Jews are left
and the area is now what is euphemistically called "inner city." To
the credit of the Society, they have not just restored buildings but
have set up their headquarters there.

Solid and serious, the Lloyd Street synagogue dates back to
1845. It is a brick building with a pediment and four large, white,
fluted columns—the neoclassical design that American builders of
that time loved to use for everything from banks to schools and
libraries or plantation houses. In boisterous contrast, the 1876 B'nai
Israel building is eclectic, flamboyant, and perhaps even a little bel-
ligerent, with pointed arch windows and Moorish flair. Joining the
synagogues is the Heritage Center, a long, low, brick building with
slightly arched openings framed inside square recesses. It links the
divergent architectural styles, if not the Judaic affiliations of the two
temples: the congregation that started what is now B'nai Israel split
off from the Lloyd Street group just thirty years after the Lloyd
Street synagogue was built. The protesters wanted to preserve orthodoxy from what they saw as rampant reform. Probably the most controversial change about to take place at the Lloyd Street synagogue

was a mixed choir of men and women. Removal of the balcony lattice work, which shielded women from view, and replacement of wax candles with gaslight were also sore points. Controversy over the perceived insults to orthodoxy was so heated that dissenting congregants filed a bill of complaint in court.

While the judge more or less sat on the complaint, protesters resigned from Lloyd Street and formed a congregation called Chizuk Amuno (see the preceding entry). The philosophical distance may have seemed vast, but the new synagogue, today's B'nai Israel, was built just down the street.

When Heritage Center was opened in 1987, the inaugural exhibit highlighted the Jewish settlement of Maryland. The inevitable effort to identify the first Jew in the colony revealed that, from the 1630s, when Maryland was founded, to the decades just before the Revolutionary War, only one Jew could be counted: Dr. Jacob Lumbrozo, who arrived from Portugal in 1656. Ironically, Lumbrozo had settled in a place where freedom of worship was protected by the Act Concerning Religion (1649), also called the Toleration Act, yet Lumbrozo was the only person ever prosecuted under that law. In truth, The Toleration Act discriminated against Jews, Quakers, and Unitarians. It read: "Whatsoever person who shall blaspheme God or deny our Savior or the Holy Trinity shall be punished with death and confiscation or forfeiture of all his or her lands."

Lumbrozo was charged with blasphemy. According to testimony against him in February 1658:

. . . being at [the] house of Mr. Richard Preston, and there meeting with Jacob Lumbrozo, he, this deponent, and the said Lumbrozo, falling into discourse concerning our Blessed Savior, Christ, his resurrection, telling [the] said Lumbrozo that he was more than man, as did appear by his resurrection. To which the said Lumbrozo answered, that his disciples stole him away. Then this deponent replied, yet no man ever did such miracles as he. To which [the] said Lumbrozo answered that such works might be done by necromancy or sorcery, or words to that purpose.

Happily, Maryland's first Jew was never brought to trial because charges against him were withdrawn under a general amnesty issued the following month. He lived a productive life of farming and business; he was a folk doctor and innkeeper, among other enterprises. Although he is recorded as the first and only Jew in Maryland before the Revolution, in his neatly handwritten will, filed in 1665, the year he died, he left his estate to his "dearly beloved wife" Elizabeth. Did she accompany him from Portugal? Wouldn't there seem to have been at least two Jews in the colony before the Revolution?

Among the valuable documents in the Society's possession are circumcision records from 1836 to 1862. However, each boy's father was listed, but not his mother, and no records of female children were kept.

In historical documentation of Jewish settlement, some patterns seem to repeat themselves, such as examples of mercantile enterprise and ingenuity. The Hendler Creamery, for instance, founded in 1905, was a model of cleanliness and efficiency. It was also, proudly, the first company to do away with hand "dipping" by packaging ice cream in individual containers. Hendler's 1920 black-and-yellow sign, an archetype of graphic design for the era, is on display at the Heritage Center.

A jug that held one of Herman Krieger's wholesale liquors can also be seen. Krieger was so successful that his business somehow managed to survive Prohibition.

Then there was Benny Goldstein, an amateur boxer in the 1920s, who didn't tell his parents about his sporting prowess when he was in high school. When the school principal revealed that Benny had missed school for a month, the truth came out. As a pro boxer, Benny Goldstein won eighty-one out of eighty-five fights. The distinctive emblem of his boxing shorts was the Star of David.

When former curator Elizabeth Kessin Berman was gathering material for the Baltimore Society's first exhibit, she came across a 19th-century painter, photographer, explorer, writer, and inventor—an artist and intellectual who intrigued her. Berman's curiosity led to the Society's second major exhibition: Solomon Nuñes Carvalho: Painter, Photographer, and Prophet in Nineteenth Century America. Unlike some other Jews who pursued the arts in the early decades of the last century, Carvalho did not turn his back on his religion.

Carvalho, born on April 27, 1815, grew up in Charleston, South Carolina, in a family of Spanish-Portuguese origin. The family had come to America via the West Indies. Carvalho worked in

הבר מצוה
יהושע קארנבלאט
שבת, בששה עשר לחדש סיון,
בבית הכנסת „חברת אנשי ספרד"

Bar mitzvah invitation of Joshua (Joseph) Kornblatt, 1916. Courtesy of the Jewish Historical Society of Maryland.

24

Photo of Benny Goldstein. Courtesy of the Jewish Historical Society of Maryland.

Philadelphia, Charleston, and Baltimore. While some historians boldly call him the first Jewish photographer in history, others hedge their bets by saying he was "one of the first." He moved from painting portraits to posing individuals for daguerreotypes. In 1853, Carvalho was explorer John C. Fremont's official artist and photographer for an expedition to the Rocky Mountains.

Communion with nature was sometimes good (". . . we reached the summit and beheld a panorama of unspeakable sublimity. . . . Above us the cerulean heaven without a single cloud to mar its beauty. . . .") and sometimes ghastly ("Alone, disabled and with no possibility of assistance from mortal man, I felt that my last hour had come; I was at the top of a mountain of snow. . . . Night approached and I looked in vain in the direction our party had proceeded. . . . Naught but a desert waste of eternal snow met my anxious gaze.").

Carvalho managed to survive the treacherous expedition, but all save one of his daguerreotype plates—well over a hundred—have been lost. He died in 1897.

❧ LEARNING EXPERIENCES ❧

THE JEWISH DISCOVERY ROOM
Board of Jewish Education
11710 Hunters Lane
Rockville, MD 20852
301-984-1611
Hours: Visits arranged by mail or telephone reservation; direct inquiries to Rita Kopin, Director.

The Discovery Room is mainly for children and has a lot of hands-on exhibits, mini-exhibits, and "discovery boxes" containing ceremonial and cultural objects, documents, and art. Visitors can look at a miniature house and seek out the objects that characterize a Jewish home, or inspect the contents of Grandmother's Trunk. An exhibit showing horns in various stages of production teaches how a shofar is made.

The Jewish Discovery Room sponsors classes for both children and adults and special programs of great variety.

❧ HAPPY NEW YEAR ❧

JANE L. AND ROBERT H. WEINER JUDAICA MUSEUM
Jewish Community Center of Greater Washington
6125 Montrose Road
Rockville, MD 20852
301-881-0100
Hours (gallery): During the school year, Monday through
Thursday, 12 to 4; Sundays, 2 to 5; Monday and Thursday
evenings, 7:30 to 9:30.

The permanent collection is in a number of display cases throughout the Community Center. These cases can be visited on any day that the building is open to the public, from 9 A.M. to 11 P.M.

The changing exhibitions are varied in size and coverage. A significant presentation organized by this museum was The Jews in the Age of Rembrandt. An impressive selection of prints was assembled from museums in this country and the Netherlands, the culmination of two years' work at the Center.

Most of the exhibits in the gallery are on loan and vary in theme. A recent show, for example, was a traveling exhibit on Blacks and Jews in the American Experience.

The permanent collection is named after Robert Weiner, former director of the JCC and a collector of Judaica who gave the Center an endowment upon his retirement.

Highlight: *A New Year's card that opens in numerous ways and shows the signatories of the First Zionist Congress, the names of biblical patriarchs, and greetings in English, Russian, and Yiddish is in the permanent collection.*

MASSACHUSETTS

❧ YIDDISH BOOKS ❧

NATIONAL YIDDISH BOOK CENTER—ADMINISTRATION
Old East Street School
South East Street
Amherst, MA 01002
413-256-1241
Hours: Monday through Friday, 9 to 5. (The Center will move
to the campus of Hampshire College, also in Amherst, sometime
in the next few years.)

NATIONAL YIDDISH BOOK CENTER ANNEX
110 Lyman Street
Holyoke, MA (no mail to this address)
413-536-0584
Hours: Monday through Friday, 9 to 4.

In 1980, an enthusiastic, optimistic, willful, and visionary young
man named Aaron Lansky realized that Yiddish, spoken and written,
had nearly vanished. That, he believed, was a tragedy because the
Yiddish language embodies the world view of a whole people. Lansky
boldly set himself an impossible goal: to save Yiddish.

By the decade's end, the National Yiddish Book Center that
Lansky started had retrieved a million volumes stored in attics,
garages, warehouses, private libraries, and even in an old hotel in the
Catskill Mountains, which was about to be torn down. Most of
these books were slated to be discarded.

Lansky's efforts have inspired over a hundred of the world's
leading libraries to participate in the Center's Yiddish Library Development Program. New courses in Yiddish, and translations from
Yiddish into English, are other developments.

As its efforts became known, the Center was offered a marvelous, unexpected windfall—85,000 folios of Jewish sheet music
that had been stored in a garage for 13 years. Among the "greatest
hits" retrieved were "Dir yidisher Yenki Dudl" (The Yiddish Yankee
Doodle) and "A yidish meydl darf a yidishn boy" (A Jewish Girl

Needs a Jewish Boy). In July 1989 (coincidentally, on the day I first stopped in to visit), it was announced that, in recognition of his efforts, Aaron Lansky had won a $225,000 MacArthur fellowship to use as he sees fit.

The mounting evidence that a major Yiddish Renaissance is under way is one of the most exciting movements in Jewish history.

Despite its ancient oral tradition, there was no serious literature in Yiddish until the latter part of the 19th century. Only Hebrew had the respect of Jewish scholars and intellectuals. Yiddish was scorned as a means of merely secular expression.

In 1864, Mendele Moykher Sforim published *Dos Kleyne Mentshele (The Little Man)*. Intended to reach the masses and tell them about the Enlightenment, it nevertheless showed artistic promise as a literary work. In the burst of populist pride that followed during the 1880s, Shalom Aleichem was among those who embraced Yiddish to tell tales and to express philosophies and social theories. For 125 years, Yiddish flourished: over 40,000 titles were published worldwide. Then the Holocaust brought the beginning of the end.

A number of important collections of Yiddish writing were secreted and smuggled out of Germany. Other private libraries came to the United States in steamer trunks, and some Yiddish writing was published in the United States for Yiddish-speaking immigrants who chose to keep their Old World language alive. Their sons and daughters, however, valued assimilation over tradition, and Yiddish was the last thing they wanted to know. The language was dying from disuse, and the books were disappearing. Among the few writers who continued to tell stories in Yiddish was Nobel prizewinner Isaac Bashevis Singer, but his words were translated into English before they were published in America.

Along came Aaron Lansky, a second-generation American. He studied Yiddish at Hampshire College, an institution that encourages the unconventional. When he went on to do graduate work at Montreal's McGill University, a major center for Jewish studies, he couldn't find Yiddish books to read. He thought about all the volumes doomed to gather mold in basements and dust in attics until they were hauled to a dump, and he felt impelled to act quickly. He solicited books through Jewish periodicals. During the first month, he was given over 3,000 volumes and he received 500 letters saying, in effect, You can have my books if you'll come and get them. In rented trucks, he set out with a group of volunteers. On one early excursion in a graffiti-covered van, their destination was a housing project apartment on New York's Lower East Side. From under the shadow of the old *Jewish Forward* building, they carried away armfuls of the works of Shalom Aleichem and Sholem Asch.

Some stories of near misses are heartbreaking. An old man in Ohio, not knowing of Lansky's efforts, tried for months to find someone who wanted his collection. At last, unable to place them or to store them any longer, he sent 9,000 books to the paper shredder! Other accounts are exhilarating and have the intrigue of some of the best Yiddish stories: libraries saved at the last moment, personal treasures that suddenly retrieve their value. The joy of people who discover the Center and know their cherished books will be read once again is as great as the excitement of the Center's collectors who have brought them to light. The goal of the Center is to get these books back into circulation. Duplicates are sold and distributed to libraries.

The Center's headquarters are in Amherst, currently in a two-story, stolid, red brick building that was formerly a school. (It will relocate to Hampshire College in the next few years.) On the second floor are small exhibitions with artifacts such as the tiny Corona typewriter with Yiddish letter-keys used by Lamed Shapiro, one of the greatest short story writers in the language. Photographs of other greats, including Isaac Lieb Peretz, a handsome man with dark eyes and a direct smile, and Shalom Aleichem, who had a goatee, a broad nose, and an intense, scholarly look, are on display.

Mostly, in both buildings of the Center, there are books. The Holyoke annex holds the largest collection of out-of-print and duplicate Yiddish volumes anywhere in the world and a newly acquired Yiddish linotype machine, believed to be the last in the world. A visit to the Center is an opportunity to get close to the extraordinary energy of the movement to rescue Yiddish culture. When Shalom Aleichem died in 1916, 150,000 mourners attended his funeral in Brooklyn. His epitaph, which he wrote himself, expresses the spirit of the Yiddish culture with which he is identified:

Here lies a simple Jew
Who wrote Yiddish tales for women;
And for the common folk
He was a humorist, a writer.
His whole life he laughed
And joined the world in its reveries.
The whole world enjoyed itself
While he—oy vey—had troubles.
And even as the public
Laughed, split their sides, whooped it up,
He grieved, as only god knows,
In secret, so that no one should see.

Highlight: *If you read Yiddish, you'll be way ahead of most visitors. Even if you can't, simple proximity to this collection seems to stir inexplicable emotions—in non-Jews as well as Jews. As you climb up to the second floor, spend time with the staircase photographs that document the adventures of Lansky and his volunteers during some of their book collection forays. There are also pictures of zamlers (volunteer book collectors) around the world who have added to the Center's volumes. Understandably, the photos all show smiling faces, except one that makes the viewer smile. In a room full of books piled nearly to the ceiling, a faceless searcher is trying to find a particular volume. What the viewer sees best are the soles of his shoes, and his trouser cuffs. The wide wall of books is supporting his body, and the tilt of his head, looking over the far edge of the wall, hints that he may just have found the title he was looking for.*

✑ COLLEGE COLLECTION ✑

HEBREW COLLEGE
43 Hawes Street
Brookline, MA 02146
617-232-8710
Hours: Monday through Thursday, 9 to 9; Friday, 9 to noon;
Sunday, 9 to 3. Hours may vary, especially during the summer.

This collection, which consists chiefly of about 100 ritual objects, began with donations to the school by the American Joint

Distribution Committee. After World War II, the Committee not only helped displaced persons but it provided relief of many kinds. Among its responsibilities was the recovery and redistribution of Jewish possessions that had been looted by the Nazis.

The Hebrew College collection is administered by the library and is kept in glass cases in various locations within the building. The main museum area is in the foyer of the Goodman building where there are three built-in and three freestanding cases. Additional cases are in the library and rare-book room.

The collection's ritual objects include silver wine goblets, spice boxes, and Torah ornaments. There are over 20 fabric articles, including Torah coverings and handmade wimples.

Special exhibits are held from time to time.

❧ THE SILVER CALF ❧

HARVARD SEMITIC MUSEUM
6 Divinity Avenue
Cambridge, MA 02138
617-495-3123
Hours: Monday through Friday, 11 to 5.

One of the Harvard Semitic Museum's most exciting archaeological finds was recently unearthed in the ancient port city of Ashkelon in southern Israel. In the summer of 1990, a Harvard Semitic Museum dig found a 4½-inch long, 3,500-year-old metal calf and the dome-shaped ceramic housing that protected it. The calf is believed to be an idol connected with worship of a Canaanite god, either El or Baal. Its bronze body was sheathed in silver.

The Silver Calf of Ashkelon, as it is already widely known and celebrated, was found on the outskirts of the city, and it is speculated that merchants approaching the city might have stopped to make an offering at the Canaanite sanctuary.

Finders is no longer keepers, however. After several months at Harvard for a celebratory exhibition, the idol was returned to its homeland, Israel.

The museum's collection is educational, with emphasis on archaeology in civilizations where the Semitic languages were spoken—

modern-day Iran, Jordan, Iraq, Syria, Lebanon, Turkey, Egypt, and Israel. What does such a collection include? A beautifully shaped pot, thousands of years old; a mummy case that sends shivers down the spine—recognizable objects that prompt the imagination. A ceramic shard with a few odd scratches will mean little to the casual visitor but represents the museum's unique value to scholars.

Nitza Rosovsky, curator at the Harvard Semitic Museum, is not an archaeologist herself but has become tuned in to what excites these historical researchers. For instance, when a member of the Near Eastern department, which oversees the museum, has been excavating on the border between Israel and Jordan and finds an inscribed article from the Bronze or Iron Age (1000 to 2000 B.C.E.)—a coin, or a jar handle—the level of enthusiasm rises significantly. Rosovsky explained:

I look at it as a piece of ceramic with a few scratches, but to scholars it opens a whole world. They say, "My God, they traded with so-and-so." In Israel, everything is made of stone. If they find a coin under a stone that has never been moved and they know when the stone was put in place, they know the date of the coin. It may not be visually exciting, but it will shed a lot of light on things for scholars.

When archaeologists look at the pottery found at different excavation levels, which represent different eras, and see changes in design, materials, or some other significant component, artistic judgments take second place to tracing the origin of the influence. Does the object's presence mean that the Egyptians invaded then? Small finds can provide important clues to how ancient peoples lived.

The life of the Harvard Semitic Museum, founded in 1889, has its own drama. It grew out of the same battle against anti-Semitism that inspired the founding of the American Jewish Historical Society, the Jewish Museum in New York City, and other educational organizations. In the late 1880s, Harvard's president was Charles W. Eliot, a man whose vision included opening the gates to students and faculty "without the least regard to their religious affiliation."

Jacob Henry Schiff, the great financier and a friend of Eliot, enthusiastically funded the new museum. Eliot's support and Schiff's money were extraordinarily productive. Early achievements included participation in the first United States expedition to the Near East (1889), the first scientific excavations in the Holy Land (Samaria, 1907–1912), and explorations at Nuzi and in the Sinai, where the earliest alphabet was found.

A. Lawrence Lowell, Eliot's successor as Harvard president in 1909, was something of a bigot. He turned attention and support away from the museum, effectively neutralizing some of the effects of Eliot's active involvement until his death in 1926. Lowell was also one of the many university administrators of that time who used the quota system as a solution to the "Jewish problem" (i.e., that Jews were increasingly making strides in academia).

Nevertheless, the collection continued to grow splendidly: thousands of clay tablets, huge models of the temples of Solomon and Herod and of the Tabernacle, and a cast of the stele of Hammurabi (ca. 2000 B.C.E.) were added. The museum was relegated to the basement during World War II when first the Army and then the Navy moved into the building. After the war, the Center for International Affairs took over the top floors. The museum work remained underground, physically if not intellectually, and most of the collection was dispersed for safekeeping.

In 1970, the roof of the building was blown off by antiwar demonstrators who targeted the Center and its military connections, especially under Henry A. Kissinger. The explosion was a dark cloud that had a silver lining because it led to the discovery of an extraordinary cache of 28,000 prints, lantern slides, and negatives—19th-century views of Middle East landscapes, architecture, and figures. Some crates had remained unopened for nearly a century.

Interest in the museum began to improve. The Harvard football team was enlisted to bring back some of the casts and bas-reliefs that were in storage off-campus. In 1978, it was announced that the Harvard Semitic Museum would come back to life.

And so it has. Since its reopening in 1982, a variety of exhibitions has featured both objects from the museum's own collections and others borrowed for short-term display. Recently, the important traveling exhibition of Judaica from the Vatican Library was followed by a fascinating show of 19th-century photographs of the Holy Land.

In time, the museum administrators hope to have a semipermanent exhibition of objects from their collection. Meanwhile, temporary exhibits will be varied, and although their breadth will be wide, there will often be an exhibition of special interest to Jewish visitors. Among the offerings, besides those noted above, have been Danzig 1939: Treasures of a Destroyed Community and Crossroads of the Ancient World: Israel's Archaeological Heritage. For Harvard's 350th anniversary in 1986, Nitza Rosovsky staged The Jewish Experience at Harvard and Radcliffe, an intriguing show, as is evident from the publication that accompanied it. In this context, the museum itself is a significant part of the story being told.

In ancient Palestine (and, until quite recently, in some present-day Israeli and Palestinian homes), clay lamps fueled with olive oil illuminated the dark of night. The museum's collection shows lamps of simple design, such as an elegant little red bowl on a stand, which has the look of a contemporary Swedish candleholder. Other lamps are elaborate—one is in the shape of a fish and is decorated with faces and scrolls and has six wick holes. My favorites are the humorous lamps: one, shaped like a human head, has an odd top knot for the handle, and an open mouth serves as a hole for the wick; another represents a mysterious pinkish animal that could be anything from a bear to a turtle. Bedecked with fancy necklaces, it sits upright, holding a container for the wick between its paws.

Highlight: *Don't miss those ancient lamps, and find as many of the Bonfils photos as you can. Beginning in 1867, members of the Bonfils family made a photographic expedition through the Holy Land that lasted for half a century. Their work, sold commercially, often has the quality of exquisite etching and captures mood as well as subject. Jewish Women in Street Costume is one of their engaging pictures of an era as well as a place, and Jewish Tin-Smith is a fond portrait of a man and his life. As you look at the Bonfils portfolio, remind yourself every now and then how, during those first years of photography, the photographer hid under a black tent while recording images on glass plates. Envision him in the desert, in a dark suit and bowler hat, and your awe at the beauty of these pictures will be increased by the knowledge of what was demanded of the person who took them.*

☙ A STORY ❧

NORTH SHORE JEWISH HISTORICAL SOCIETY
31 Exchange Street
Lynn, MA 01901
617-593-2386
Hours: By appointment. A call left on the answering machine will
be returned.

The North Shore Jewish Historical Society was founded during
the 1976 American Bicentennial. The goal of the Society, like most
historical societies, is to preserve local history and mount exhibitions that detail that history. Locally, the North Shore means the
coastal area of Massachusetts above Boston.

Among exhibits assembled in the past were Notable Artists of
the North Shore and Living and Working in the Old Neighbor-
hoods of Lynn.

The collection includes documents and minutes of local synagogues, Hadassah, and Jewish Athletes of the North Shore, and
enlarged photos of local places, people, and events.

In the Society's brochure are wonderful turn-of-the-century
photos—a bride and groom, a little girl in shiny Mary Janes with a big
bow in her hair, a factory scene—and a quotation from Irving Howe
that says it all: "A story is the essential unit of our life, offering the
magical imperatives of 'so it began' and 'so it came to an end.' A story
encompasses us, justifies our stay, prepares our leaving."

☙ ON CAMPUS ❧

STARR GALLERY
Leventhal-Sidman Jewish Community Center on the Gosman Campus
333 Nahanton Street
Newton Centre, MA 02159
617-965-7410, ext. 168
Hours: Monday through Thursday, 10 to 4; Friday, 10 to 2; Sunday,
11 to 4; Tuesday and Wednesday evenings, 6 to 9.

When I visited this gallery, there was a wonderful exhibition of
prints, watercolors, drawings, and sculptures of animals by contem-

porary artists. The gallery has an interesting program of exhibitions, from Judaica such as Hanukkah windows to non-Jewish themes by Jewish artists.

The Gosman Campus is a compound that includes a number of Jewish organizations (such as Jewish Family Services). The gallery is close to the main entrance of a high-energy Jewish Community Center and it is fun to tour the facilities.

❧ AMERICAN, NOT SECTARIAN ❧

AMERICAN JEWISH HISTORICAL SOCIETY
Two Thornton Road
Waltham, MA 02154
617-891-8110
Hours: Monday through Friday, 8:30 to 5; Sundays (only during
the academic year), 2 to 5.

The history of the American Jewish Historical Society is itself a lively tale. It begins in the 19th century, just after the Civil War. With a new sense of nationalism, Americans, including about 2,000 Jews mainly of German origin, began to resent the influx of immigrants. Comfortably settled across the country, successful, and feeling assimilated, those Jews became dismayed when Russian and Rumanian Jews, fleeing persecution, began arriving in droves. During a period of 20 years, beginning in the 1880s, 2.5 million Eastern Europeans emigrated to America. The Jewish Establishment was mortified: the new immigrants spoke loudly, dressed strangely, and seemed uncouth to the Old Guard, who blamed them for the growing anti-Semitism. Their solution was education. At one of the first organizational meetings of what would become the American Jewish Historical Society, this impassioned statement was made by Dr. Charles Gross, Professor of History at Harvard:

The object of this society will be to reveal what the Jews have done. It will be made evident that the Jews of this country have been ready to offer up life and fortune for this country, that they have been patriots in time of war and philanthropists in time of peace and that they will be

*patriots and philanthropists in the future as they have been in the past,
and as they are in the present. If we can once make that plain through
the researches of the society, it seems to me we will accomplish a great
deal to elevate the position of the Jews in America and to dispel
prejudice.*

Though the aim was clear, controversy raged over decisions such
as how far beyond American Jewry the research should go, how much
overlap with other organizations should be avoided, whether the
scope of activities should be "limited" or "universal," and whether a
rabbi should be on the executive council. Disputes threatened the
very existence of the new organization, as even *The New York Times*
reported. Finally, calm returned, and, at the first official meeting
of the American Jewish Historical Society (AJHS), in December 1892,
the elected president, Oscar S. Straus, told his audience: "The objects
of our Society . . . are not sectarian, but American."

When Straus left the country to become America's minister to
Turkey in 1898, Cyrus Adler took his place. A renowned and active
scholar, Adler was also involved in the governance of so many organizations, including the Jewish Theological Seminary and Dropsie
College, that, when asked what her father did for a living, his young
daughter replied that he was a president. In 1903, the AJHS established its headquarters at the new Seminary in New York City,
where books, manuscripts, and other collections were stored.

The financial fortunes of the AJHS began to slide in the 1930s
and 1940s. Then came the presidency of Lee M. Friedman in 1948.
Friedman was a successful corporation lawyer and an avid historian.
The flavor of AJHS writings became more scholarly and had a revi-
sionist approach during his tenure. When Friedman died nearly 10
years later, leaving his estate to the AJHS, its economic well-being
improved, though not without a renewal of conflict.

With money available for a new building to house the treasures
and staff functions, the divisive question was where to locate it. Some
members were adamant that it should stay in New York; others were
equally insistent on a move to Philadelphia. The disagreement got so
bad that the contenders went to court. Gossipers said that the judge
recommended that all parties go out to a restaurant, have a good meal
and a few drinks, and settle out-of-court. When land owned by

Brandeis University was offered, the problem was solved by default rather than consensus. The AJHS moved to Waltham in 1968.

Today, virtually on the Brandeis campus but independent of the university, the American Jewish Historical Society is in a two-story concrete building, in a quiet, shaded spot on the edge of the campus, simultaneously part and apart, as Jews have been forever. The ambience is open and accessible, and the collection is available to researchers, or "readers" as librarian Nathan Kaganoff (known among the staff as "Dr. K") calls them. Brimming with knowledge and humor, Dr. K, who studied Jewish history as a Korean War veteran under the G.I. Bill, has worked for the AJHS since he graduated. He says the AJHS serves around 900 to 1,000 readers, answers about 800 letters asking for information, and welcomes more than 2,000 visitors to the collection every year.

Besides books, the AJHS collection includes paintings, heirlooms of descendants of early American Jewish families (for example, the wedding gown worn by Miriam Peizotto Davis when she married Michael Marks in 1866), and a silk banner carried in 1889 in the New York centennial celebration of the inauguration of President Washington. On the front is a representation of George Washington, enclosed within an embroidered border; on the reverse is the inscription "Awarded to the Hebrew Benevolent and Orphan Asylum Society of the City of New York for fine bearing in the Civic and Industrial Parade." The Society also displays evidence of a darker side of Jewish life in America—sheet music like "The Sheeny Coon."

A few areas are sectioned off for small exhibitions, usually of material drawn from the collection. When I visited, one exhibition was of portraits, miniatures, daguerreotypes, and silhouettes ranging from the Colonial period through the 19th century. There was also a display of Yiddish Theater material from the AJH's very extensive collection.

There are more biographies on the bookshelves than any other types of books. Among them are 20 to 30 books about Christopher Columbus.

Every six months, Dr. K makes a list of new works of scholarship in the field that is most aptly called the American-Jewish experience; on every list are between 200 and 250 new titles. For this oldest continuously operating ethnic historical society in America, one that has thrived in spite of controversy, the field remains energetic and exciting.

Highlight: *Some excellent Colonial portraits in this collection shouldn't be missed. True to the style of the itinerant painters of the first half of the 18th century, the unknown artists represented here endeavored to place their subjects in the appropriate surroundings so that viewers would immediately be able to say, by virtue of the fine silk collar, the velvet drapes, and the sailing ship outside the window, "Here is a wealthy man who is probably in the import business." Not so obvious is the situation of an elegant woman with dark, almond eyes, whose dress has a voluminous skirt and who looks demure despite the low cut of her gown. Until you read about her, you will not know that she was utterly mortified when her daughter married a gentile. "Good God what a shock it was when they acquainted me she had left the house and had bin [sic] married six months. I can hardly hold my pen whilst I am writing it," she said in a letter to her son.*

🙚 MOROCCAN WEDDING 🙘

WORCESTER ART MUSEUM
55 Salisbury Street
Worcester, MA 01609-3196
508-799-4406
Hours: Tuesday, Wednesday, and Friday, 11 to 4; Thursday, 11 to 8; Saturday, 10 to 5; Sunday, 1 to 5.

Eugene Delacroix went to Morocco as a member of the French diplomatic mission in 1832, and the trip inspired some of his best work. The artist was most excited by the scene of a Jewish wedding in Tangier. He noted and sketched the musicians who, seated on rugs on the floor of a courtyard, played a three-stringed violin, a guitar, and a tambourine. Dancers came in one-by-one, twirling their skirts and silk scarves slowly at first, then faster and faster. The courtyard was filled with celebrants—Moors who wore turbans, light colored clothes, and bright yellow slippers, and Jews in somber black or dark blue garments with broad brown belts, black slippers,

The Jewish Wedding (after Delacroix) by Pierre-Auguste Renoir. Courtesy of Worcester Art Museum.

and skull caps. The bride was missing; she stayed in her room until later in the festivities.

Delacroix's painting of *The Jewish Wedding* has hung in the Louvre since 1874. Though Paris is out of the range of this book, the painting can be seen in Worcester, Massachusetts. It is a copy, true, but done by none other than Renoir! He was commissioned to paint the copy by a patron. Renoir the Impressionist greatly admired Delacroix the Romantic, and he reproduced the masterwork in 1875 or 1876 with care and affection. It was bought by the Worcester Museum in 1943.

Besides the opportunity of seeing an important work by a master artist, Renoir's *The Jewish Wedding* offers a context of wedding costumes, jewelry, and other objects found in Judaica collections.

❧ EARLY AMERICAN ❧

AMERICAN ANTIQUARIAN SOCIETY
185 Salisbury Street
Worcester, MA 01609
508-755-5221
Hours: Monday through Friday, 9 to 5.

This organization, founded in 1812, is an independent research library. The collection is available for graduate and postdoctoral work. Students need a letter of introduction from the faculty member overseeing their project, and other adults need two forms of identification. Significant material on the Jews in America during the 18th and 19th centuries is housed here, including helpful information for genealogical research.

A few years ago, the Society held an exhibition, drawn from its holdings, on the impact of Jews in the North American colonies. These are some of the items they showed:

- The first Hebrew Bible printed in America, in 1814.
- A number of Hebrew grammars, compiled by Americans, for the use of divinity students.
- A copy of the regimental handbook of the 9th Regiment, New York Artillery. Aaron Levy, a New York merchant, was a staunch member of the regiment and fought with it during the War of 1812. Two years before he retired, he compiled the handbook.
- A Fourth of July oration by Mordecai Manuel Noah, in which he contrasted the freedom Jews have in America with their lack of freedom in Europe. Noah grew up in Philadelphia and, after the War of 1812, settled in New York. This discourse was delivered at the consecration of a synagogue in New York.
- Three of Samuel B. H. Judah's publications: *The Buccaneers, Gotham and the Gothamites,* and *A Tale of Lexington, a National Comedy.* Judah became a renowned playwright at a young age. The publication in 1827 of *Gotham and the*

Gothamites, a scurrilous attack on New York City politicians, landed him in jail for libel. Judah thought very little of Mordecai Manuel Noah, and made that clear in print.

- A copy of a tract published in 1669, the first in a series, in which the well-known Colonial minister Increase Mather made public his convictions on the conversion of Jews. Throughout the late 17th and 18th centuries, sermons were preached on the desirability of Jews converting to Christianity.

- The only printed sermon by Rabbi Karigal, who came to Newport via Jerusalem (his birthplace), Europe, South America, and the West Indies. It is entitled *The Salvation of Israel* and was preached, in Touro, in 1773.

NEW YORK

🍃 BITTER HOPE 🍃

THE NEW YORK STATE MUSEUM
Empire State Plaza
Albany, NY 12230
518-474-5877
Hours: Daily, 10 to 5.

In a beautiful marble building across from the State Capitol on Empire State Plaza (a project of former Governor Nelson A. Rockefeller) is the New York State Museum, the first and still one of the finest state museums in the country. Exhibits illuminate zoology, botany, geology, paleontology, anthropology, and gemology. A million or more people go through this museum every year and see dioramas devoted to subjects like the Native Peoples of New York, the Adirondack Wilderness, and the Big Apple. The museum's New York Metropolis Hall examines the urbanization of the ultimate urban region.

Visitors who pass through Metropolis Hall may well be surprised to find themselves in an exhibit called Bitter Hope: From Holocaust to Haven. Created for the museum through a legislative grant, this exhibit documents a strange, little known event. In July 1944, 982 victims of the Nazi Holocaust left Europe in anticipation of finding freedom in America. Eighteen nationalities were represented, and there were 874 Jews, 73 Roman Catholics, 28 Orthodox Greeks, and 7 Protestants. President Franklin Delano Roosevelt had announced in January of that year that the refugees would be "guests of the President" for the duration of the war. Instead, when they arrived, they found themselves virtual prisoners, quarantined in a camp at Fort Ontario in Oswego, New York.

They were not allowed outside the camp grounds for more than six hours at a time. Their mail was censored. Their detention in Oswego until the fall of 1945 is a dreadful but relevant piece of American history.

An iron cot, personal notebooks, and photographs are some of the surviving items on display. Photographs taken at the camp show a group of toddlers holding hands in front of the white clapboard barracks, people lining up for supplies, and a wedding under a chupa, a ceremonial canopy.

When the exhibition premiered in January 1986, almost 30 of the camp's former inhabitants were able to attend the opening. "It's me, it's me," whispered Dr. Adam Munz when he looked at a photograph of a 15-year-old boy.

"I hid in a convent for nine months," a woman told a reporter. She opened her purse and took out the false papers identifying her as a Christian, which had saved her life. Later, she presented the papers to the museum.

Interesting and moving, the exhibition also has its amusing ironies. There is, for instance, the story of Nandor Segore's gold watch. Segore lost his watch when he was deported to Auschwitz. Twenty-seven years later, a man walked into the Albany jewelry shop of Segore's son, Anton, asking for an appraisal. When questioned about the watch, the man fled. The watch was on display when the exhibit opened. It isn't there now, but you will see a photo of its rightful owner and his family.

Highlight: *Norma Ball visited Fort Ontario when she was beginning her work as project administrator for the Bitter Hope exhibit. It happened to be a beautiful spring day and a gentle breeze blew across Lake Ontario, but she could imagine how cold that wind would become in winter. As she stood on a hill looking down at the site of the camp, she saw a piece of its chain link fence.*

Today, the fence is part of the exhibit; a blown-up photo of the camp street, taken during the period of internment, has been placed behind it. On the exhibit's opening night, the refugees of long ago approached the fence with a kind of quiet reverence, almost as if they had come to the Wailing Wall in Jerusalem.

When she takes school groups through the exhibit, Ball uses the fence to exemplify moral responsibility. "Watch out for fences being put up around people," she says. "And when you see such fences going up, be sure to tear them down."

And Still They Waited

By 1942, the Allies had clear evidence that the *"final solution"*— extermination of the Jews—was a fact. And still no country came forward to act as even a temporary haven for refugees fleeing Nazi terror. In the United States immigration quotas were less than 50% filled, while thousands fled, hid, or died. Economic depression and national security fears were at the core of this illogic, as well as the stain of anti-Semitism.

Käthe Kollwitz *"Grain for Sowing Shall Not Be Milled"*

Reproduction Courtesy of THE GALERIE ST. ETIENNE New York, N.Y.

"It takes months and months to grant a visa, and then it usually applies to a corpse... The time to act is long past due."

Congressman Emanuel Celler, November 1943

In the first months of 1944, as the Allied armies liberated the towns and cities of southern Italy, refugees poured in from the Nazi- where they had hidden for so long. Few had they flooded the roads

A work by Kathe Kollwitz expresses the pain and terror of refugees. At the New York State Museum.

Photo of 15-year-old Adam Munz. At the New York State Museum.

Photo of the fence encircling the camp at Fort Ontario taken through a piece of the fence itself. At the New York State Museum.

☙ INSPIRATION AND ENJOYMENT ❧

THE JUDAICA MUSEUM
The Hebrew Home for the Aged at Riverdale
5961 Palisade Avenue
Bronx, NY 10471
212-548-1006
Hours: Monday through Thursday, 1 to 4:30; Sunday, 1 to 5.

Museums often have trouble identifying, contacting, appealing to, and serving their potential audience. Not this one.

When businessman Ralph Baum and his wife, Leuba, gave their collection of Judaica to the Hebrew Home for the Aged at Riverdale, they made a wise decision. The Baum treasures are now accessible to people for whom they have a particular resonance. The Home, a complex of apartment buildings housing over 1,000 residents on 19 acres overlooking the Hudson River, provides a built-in audience.

The museum is part of Riverhouse West, a residence for elderly people who can still operate independently. Less self-sufficient residents of the Home are included in programs, as are members of the larger, surrounding community. In fact, the museum programs and exhibits touch the lives of many, young and old, in the area.

Although their resolution was unusual, the particular circumstances that brought the Baum holdings here are not. The Baums wanted to be sure their collection would be kept intact. Large museums, such as the Jewish Museum, would not guarantee that; Jacob Reingold, director of the Home, did. He is a collector himself and he has filled the corridors of the Home's residences with works of art. The appropriateness of having the Baums' Judaica at the Bronx site did not escape Reingold. He secured funds to house it, and the museum, an addition to a preexisting building, opened in 1982.

Ralph Baum left Germany in 1936. "Seeing the handwriting on the wall," he later wrote, "I resolved to gather and collect objects pertaining to the world and life soon to be destroyed. But, it was not until years later that I could afford to start the collection of Judaica that now numbers over 800 items and is regarded as one of the finest of its kind in private hands."

Among these rare and beautiful objects are candlesticks, lamps, covers for the Hallah, special Sabbath knives, kiddush cups, spice boxes, a shofar, and many other items that mark Jewish ceremonies and holidays. One very large bronze synagogue lamp, dated 1750, has a symbolic Polish eagle on top, and a very small metal amulet has been traced to the 12th century. One of the most moving items is a Torah scroll that has no special antiquity or craftsmanship, but had been in the synagogue where Ralph Baum's father was a rabbi before World War II.

The synagogue, in a suburb of Hamburg, was destroyed and the Torah ark was burned during Kristallnacht, November 9-10, 1938. When Baum went to Germany after the war, he discovered that the charred and water-damaged scroll still existed, after being kept for years in the local police station. He rescued it, brought it home, and it is now in this museum.

Ralph Baum died in 1982, but his words still serve to introduce the collection:

The museum was created to insure that Jewish traditions and customs would not be forgotten. I hope that our visitors and friends will find inspiration and enjoyment in viewing the exhibit. The museum is far away from the hustle and bustle of the big city. We hope that this will give the visitors an opportunity to relax, reflect, reminisce and find solace amid memories.

Highlight: *Many of the people who live at the Hebrew Home for the Aged probably once decorated the walls of their own homes with works of art. It is their great fortune that the director of the Home is a man who knows the value of covering the walls of the institution with works by Picasso, Marc Chagall, Andy Warhol, Alexander Calder, and Frank Stella, among others. Not only is the art an acknowledgment of the people who are now residents or patients at the Home, but it is also an inspiration to the staff who works there. A group of housekeepers from a Portuguese background, for instance, supported the purchase of a work by a Portuguese artist. As the Home's director of recreation and arts once told a reporter, "I love working in a place that is beautiful."*

✎ THE STAR ✑

JUDAIC MUSEUM OF TEMPLE BETH ZION
Benjamin and Dr. Edgar R. Cofeld
805 Delaware Avenue
Buffalo, NY 14209-2095
716-886-7150
Hours: Monday through Friday, 9 to 5; Saturday, 10 to 2.

In a simple frame, on a dark background, is a small yellow star with the word Jude in the center. Johanna Stern wore it while she was in the Terezin concentration camp during World War II. Today, this small cotton emblem of the unspeakable is displayed as honorably as if it were carved in gold. Its recent history has curious beginnings.

In primitive art, the six-point star formed by double triangles, which we call the Star of David, represented life. The single apex pointing upward symbolized the female, and the one pointing downward, the male.

In early Christianity, the points signified God, World, Man, Creation, Revelation, and Redemption.

Ancient Arabs and Jews used the sign in magic and cabalistic practices, believing it had power over demons.

During the 17th century, in alchemy, the star showed the synthesis of fire and water. This harmonious resolution of opposing tendencies represented the struggle to achieve order among diverse and opposing forces, and so it alluded to the possibility of reuniting these forces with the center, around which all else revolves. The star is thus an unusual Western version of the Oriental mandela.

Because the star also signified distillation, it was used as a sign on brandy shops in medieval times. (On the label of Mogen David wine, it still is.)

Distillation is not its primary symbolism in the Jewish world today; it now represents both Israel and worldwide Judaism. The history of the Magen David (literally, shield of David; also known as the seal of Solomon) is uncertain. An early official use of the Magen David as a Jewish symbol came about in 1354 when Emperor Charles IV allowed the Jews of Prague to have their own flag. The Star of David became part of the official seal of the Jewish community of

Prague. From there, it spread through Europe and became the symbol of the Zionist movement at the end of the 19th century.

Because it was so widely synonymous with Judaism, the Star of David was used by the Nazis to identify Jews, many of whom went to the death chambers wearing the symbol. Rather than hide their religion, even during the Nazi regime, many Jews wore their stars boldly, transforming a symbol of disaster into an emblem of pride.

Allies in Holland also wore the Magen David badge to demonstrate their solidarity with the persecuted Jews. In 1942, the Dutch Underground printed and distributed 300,000 replicas of the badge, inscribed: "Jews and non-Jews stand united in their struggle."

The Danish king, Christian X, also courageously defied the Nazis and wore the badge himself.

Today, the Star of David stands for the noblest traits of human character—courage, pride, survival, and hope. Happily, Johanna Stern's yellow star left Terezin when she did. Mrs. Stern died at the age of 92 in Israel.

The Star of David in this museum takes its place among a varied, comprehensive collection. The oldest object is a capital from a 10th-century Torah ark. It is made of gilded gesso over wood and was brought here from a Yugoslavian synagogue where it was found tucked away in storage.

Silver kiddush cups from the 19th and early 20th centuries run from simple and elegant to elaborately ornamental. Spice containers, candlesticks, coins, and medallions are arranged in freestanding and wall cases.

The shofars on display vary greatly in shape and color. Most are, indeed, rams' horns. An exception is a 20th-century shofar from Yemen, fashioned from a gray and black antelope horn. Hollowed-out horns are heated and then shaped. In Biblical times, the shofar was sounded on ceremonial occasions such as the anointing of kings, the proclamation of wars, the signing of peace treaties, and, still familiar to congregants, the ushering in of the festivals and the Sabbath. It is believed that the prophet Elijah will announce the coming of the Messiah by sounding the great shofar of Redemption.

A large silver ring from Morocco represents an interesting custom that first appeared in the 16th century. The ring belonged to the Jewish community. When a woman was wed, she wore the ring for the first weeks of her marriage and then returned it to the communal safe.

Highlight: *Among memorabilia are pages from Buffalo newspapers dated October 5, 1961. "Temple Beth Zion Destroyed by Fire" was one banner headline, and a picture spread showed the destruction. Other headlines softened the blow: "Help Lifts Spirits of the Congregation. . ." "Beth Zion Ashes Grow Cold; But the Fire of Faith Burns On"; "Firefighter Risks Life to Save Torah."*

The lost building was a great domed Byzantine structure with turrets, a cobbled stone exterior, and small, deep-set windows. It had been dedicated in September 1890.

The new temple, finished in 1966, is a brilliant design by Max Abramovitz. The encircling stone walls have 10 scallops representing the Ten Commandments. The west wall of the sanctuary, designed by Ben Shahn, was inspired by the 150th Psalm: Hallelujah: Praise God in His Sanctuary. . . .

◄ NOAH ►

GRAND ISLAND CORNERSTONE AT THE BUFFALO AND ERIE COUNTY HISTORICAL SOCIETY
25 Nottingham Court
Buffalo, NY 14216
716-873-9644
Hours: Tuesday through Saturday, 10 to 5; Sunday, 12 to 5.

Mordecai Manuel Noah was the first native-born Jew to achieve national prominence. During his career, he secured an appointment as Consul to the Kingdom of Tunis by persuading Secretary of State Robert Smith and President James Madison that they would particularly benefit by naming a Jew to that position, thereby showing foreigners that religion was no bar to government service in this country. It would, he suggested, bring more Jews and more of their money to the United States.

Unhappily, Noah's mission to Tunis, around 1813, ended badly. A nasty letter, written by then Secretary of State James Monroe said, "At the time of your appointment, as Consul to Tunis, it was not known that the religion which you profess would form any obstacle to the exercise of your Consular functions." The reason for Noah's disgrace is somewhat fuzzy, but it has been suggested that his mission to secure the release of American captives backfired and that he paid too much money for too few prisoners—and the wrong ones at that.

Noah protested publicly and had his supporters, but his career in the foreign service was ended. He rebounded, and was later active as a journalist, a sheriff, a playwright, and a publisher. He was also a visionary who tried to establish a homeland for Jews in New York State. Noah secured some land on Grand Island, near Buffalo, in 1825. He named it Ararat, after the site where the ancient Noah's ark came safely to rest.

On September 15, 1825, Noah, dressed in crimson robes trimmed with ermine, led a ceremony proclaiming Grand Island "A City of Refuge for the Jews." The ceremony was not conducted on the island because Noah was unable to assemble the requisite transportation. A band played the grand march from "Judas Maccabeus," cannons boomed, there was a parade to the local church, speakers urged Jewish immigration to Ararat, and a monument, with lettering in Hebrew and English commemorating the event, was dedicated. "In this free and happy country," Noah said, "distinctions in religion are unknown; here we enjoy liberty without licentiousness, and land without oppression."

Noah's scheme drew more ridicule than support. The Grand Island sanctuary for Jews never materialized, the cornerstone was never laid, no monument was built, and the scheme evaporated.

But the cornerstone still exists and is now the property of the Buffalo Historical Society. As museum items go, it is a hot property that is much requested for various exhibitions. It has been traveling around the country, but is expected back in Buffalo in 1992. If you plan a trip to see it, call the Historical Society first.

❧ CHECKMATE ❧

THE CORNING MUSEUM OF GLASS
One Museum Way
Corning, NY 14830-2253
607-974-8271
Hours: Daily, 9 to 5.

The Corning Museum is to glass as a textbook is to knowledge: it starts with the beginning, moves up to date, and even projects into the future. The collection is altogether fabulous, but, at one display case, I did a double take. Did I really see what I saw?

Yes, it *was* a glass chess set, but not the standard kings, queens, bishops, knights, castles, and pawns. In this set, the opposing ranks represented Christians and Jews.

The concept was a touch impious, perhaps, but all the more amusing. The figures were whimsical, humorous, finely detailed, and very animated. Medieval Christians are represented with a bishop figure as the standard chess "king." The "queen," her hands clasped in prayer and head bowed, is an abbess; the "castle" pieces are acolytes; and so it goes.

The artist who created this send-up, Gianni Toso, is an Orthodox Jew, so it is no surprise that he put a great deal more attention into the representation of the Jewish figures, all of whom wear their prayer shawls with panache. The "king" piece is a rabbi, the "queen"

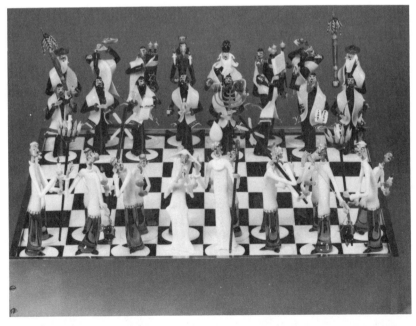

Chess set by Gianni Toso (1981). Courtesy of the Corning Museum of Glass, Corning, New York.

holds Sabbath lights, the figures that would ordinarily be "bishops" are carrying the Torah, and the "knights" are blowing shofars. For "castle" pieces, figures carry tall palm branches (lulav)—and other greens.

Toso was born in Italy in 1942. His family has been in the glass-blowing trade for 400 years. He started working at age 10 in a glass foundry in Venice. Now renowned for his work, he began creating his hasidim chess figures in 1962. A rabbi who was a chess maven planted the idea in his head. Toso has also created genre scenes of Jewish celebration in glass, including a wedding under a chupa and a succoth festival. Boisterous and colorful, his works inevitably bring a smile to visitors' faces.

At the Corning Museum, you may want to look for three other pieces in the Jewish tradition. The oldest dates from 300 to 500 years B.C.E. and is probably from Syria: a small bottle, no more than 4½ inches high and 3½ inches in diameter, octagonal in shape, and made of amber glass with a "peacock" iridescence. Old Testament symbols, including a tree of life and a menorah, are used in its decoration. The bottle came from the collection of J. P. Morgan and has been on exhibit at the Metropolitan Museum of Art. It is believed that this little bottle was used in ancient times to fulfill the ritual of washing the hands before eating.

A 1796 English wine glass is inscribed with Hebrew lettering that begins: "I want to lift this goblet and invoke the name of the Everlasting God on the feast of the circumcision of my beloved son. . . ."

A Bohemian beaker from the 19th century is inscribed in Yiddish with a forget-me-not and, on the other side, a black fly!

❧ TOUCH TV ❧

AMERICAN MUSEUM OF NATURAL HISTORY
Central Park West at 79th Street
New York, NY 10024-5192
212-769-5100 (general information)
212-769-5000 (offices)
Hours: Daily, 10 to 5:45; Friday and Saturday, 10 to 9.

On the second floor, past the Asiatic mammals, in the Hall of Asian Peoples, is an unusual exhibition that opened in 1989—a history of the Jews of Asia, which follows their chronology in the context of early civilizations of Sumeria, Babylon, and Egypt.

On one wall is a television screen that responds to touch (an interactive TV, in current museum lingo). When first touched, the screen presents a map from which various countries can be selected—Turkey, Syria, Lebanon, Iraq, India, and so on.

I called up information about India. According to legend, Jewish settlers in India were refugees from the Holy Land who were shipwrecked off India's southwest coast in the 2nd century B.C.E. Local villagers offered them shelter. The first documented population of Jews in India was in Cochin, during the 11th century. Successive waves of immigration to India were from Spain, Portugal, and Holland. With the growth of British trading companies during the 18th and 19th centuries, a large number of Jews moved to Bombay and, interestingly, one of their chief occupations was pressing coconut oil. As British influence grew in India, many Jews became doctors and lawyers.

On a wall next to the TV screen is a hand-painted ketubah from 1869. Originating from Tehran, Persia (today's Iran), it has a colorful Islamic design, and is written in Aramaic and Judeo-Persian dialect. The translation begins: "The handsome bridegroom, dear Ezra, son of the late father Ya'akov Katz. . . ." It goes on with what we consider today quaint phrasing, such as "And thus said the bridegroom," and enumerates the husband's responsibilities.

A long display on a wall facing the screen is a time line that uses both artifacts—a miniature Torah, a scribe's box, a long shofar—and small pictures of Jews. The historical grid marks important moments in Asian-Jewish history, beginning with the Babylonian exile of the 6th century B.C.E. The fate of Jews is followed as they moved into Turkey, China, India, Afghanistan, Yemen, and other areas, and there are auspicious quotations from people such as one 1st-century B.C.E. settler in Israel who said: "What a privilege to live here under Roman rule! Caesar has rebuilt the walls of Jerusalem and exempted us from a law—required of other subjects—to worship him as a deity."

Highlight: *In a small diorama near the history of the Asian Jews is a model representing a part of the ancient Babylonian city of Ur, on the Euphrates River. Ur was the home of Abraham, and the site from which he began his travels along the Fertile Crescent to the Promised Land.*

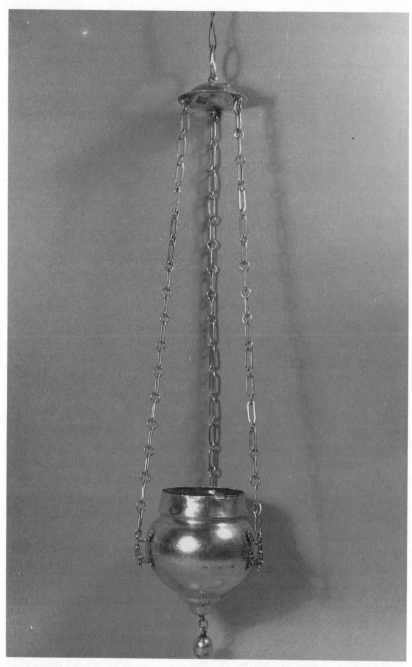

Silver eternal lamp, suspended by chains, with matching canopy. Lebanon, early 20th century. Courtesy of American Museum of Natural History.

Bronze Torah pointer used to guide readers in following the sacred Torah text. Syria, ca. 1850. Courtesy of American Museum of Natural History.

🥬 FOR THE CHILDREN 🥬

**A LIVING MEMORIAL TO THE HOLOCAUST—MUSEUM OF
JEWISH HERITAGE**
Battery Park City
Temporary address: 342 Madison Avenue, Suite 706
New York, NY 10173
212-687-9141
Hours: Opening date (1993) to be announced.

*At the end of the war, I wanted to go to the highest place I could
find and say "No more war!" At first I thought no one would ever
know it happened, or remember the people who died. Now, in 1988,
there is starting to come a voice, and something will remain, and the
children's children will know. . . .*

Ella Freilich of the Bronx was giving to the Holocaust Museum
the rough wool, blue-and-gray-striped prison uniform that she had
worn as a young woman, when she had been interned in three Nazi
concentration camps.

At the museum is another dress, from Dachau. This one, of
cotton fabric that has small blue checks instead of wide blue stripes,
has a gathered skirt and puffed sleeves. "To me it's the most beautiful dress in the world," Frania Blum explains. "I call it my liberation
dress." She sewed it from the cloth brought by American soldiers
when they freed inmates at Dachau.

Tangible objects such as the brass trumpet that Louis Bannet
had to play while others marched to their death; the yellow stars
European Jews were forced to wear; the photographs and scrap-
books—these are among the mementos that give face and form to
the past. The past explored in the museum's collection also predate
the Nazis, with household and ritual objects from prewar Europe,
such as bookbinders' tools, charity boxes, and scheren schnitten
(elaborate paper cutouts). Prewar Jewish settlement in America will
be recollected with a sweatshop sewing machine, Yiddish theater
posters, and a pamphlet concerning U.S. citizenship, written in Yiddish, produced by the Daughters of the American Revolution.

A photograph, dated c. 1937, shows 13 dancers, in shorts,
spread on the floor to shape a scallop shell. Their feet are at

Dance students at Judith Berg's school in Warsaw, circa 1937. Gift of Felix Firbich. Courtesy of Museum of Jewish Heritage, New York, scheduled to open in 1994.

the center, and their heads are positioned to form a semicircle. The picture was taken in Warsaw at the studio of Judith Berg, a well-known dancer and choreographer who developed a style of dance that used Jewish ritual movement and gesture for inspiration and drew upon Jewish folklore and literature for themes. Most of the dancers in the photograph perished, but Judith Berg and Felix Firbich, her partner, escaped. In the museum's holdings is a large collection of materials spanning 50 years of dance and documenting the extraordinary Felix Firbich Dance Company: costume designs for dances they created, photographs taken in their studios before and after the war, letters, and documents.

Highlight: *"You see, young people today, they want to have their heroes, they want to have people to look up to," said Rudy Blatt. "It's the young people who have to know how to stand up in the future, how to fight back. They have to know that if we stand up, people have to respect us, and sometimes respect turns into admiration." During the war, Blatt was in the Dutch resistance movement, for which he received numerous commendations and awards. He has given the Holocaust Museum the armband that Dutch resistance fighters wore so proudly after Holland was liberated. Blatt is a hero. The children's children will know about him.*

✺ GRAND CENTRAL SYNAGOGUE ✺

COMMUNITY HOUSE
Central Synagogue
123 East 55th Street
New York, NY 10022
212-838-5122
Hours: Monday through Friday, 9 to 5.

At Lexington Avenue and 55th Street is a neo-Moorish temple, its towers defiantly reaching toward heaven even though they are dwarfed by even the city's smallest skyscrapers. Central Synagogue was built in the 1870s. Its light, multicolored stone facade sets off a decorative round window and deep-set arches. This historic landmark is one of New York's oldest, richest, and most beautiful houses of worship. The congregation joined the Reform movement in 1873, a few years after it was founded. The synagogue has an outstanding Judaica collection that is exhibited in the Community House lobby, across 55th Street from the synagogue.

Exceptional items in this collection include silver spice containers that have a touch of fantasy. One is a fish with ruby eyes and etched scales. Another fish's head and fin are silver but its body is glass, and through the glass one can see the cinnamon and cloves it holds.

Several beautiful Torah shields and crowns from Eastern and Western Europe are in the collection. Some are extravagantly ornamented, others are more subdued.

In the hall on the fourth floor, a 19th-century German wall hanging shows heroic Queen Esther, who saved her people from wicked Haman. Esther is pictured presenting her uncle, Mordecai, to King Ahasuerus. The figures in the courtly scene are done in needlepoint with silk and velvet appliqué, silk and metallic embroidery, and beading.

In the library, on the same floor, in stark contrast to the needlepoint but also from mid-19th-century Germany, is a painted linen Passover banner in a more folklike tradition. Inside a circle formed by a Hebrew inscription from the Haggadah, Adam and Eve stand beneath a stylized apple tree. The tree is topped by an enormous bird whose wingspread equals the width of the tree's canopy. The wily serpent, curled above Eve's head, seems to be dropping an apple on her forehead, and she is handing another apple to Adam. Poor Eve looks like an old crone. The couple is surrounded by a panoply of miscellaneous birds and beasts, lions to peacocks, and they all appear to be slightly startled, as if they can't believe what's going on. This irresistible bit of artistry was hung on the wall as decoration during the Passover holiday.

Highlight: *In the synagogue ark itself, there are five Torah scrolls, four in crimson mantles and one in a heavily brocaded cover. Several have ornamental finials.*

The ark, made of cherry and oak and carved, gilded, and painted, is Islamic in style. Its doors are open during worship and one scroll is removed for Torah readings, except on the holiday of the giving of the Law (Simhat Torah), when all are taken out and carried around the synagogue in procession. Visitors should try to attend a service to see these beautiful Torahs. Alternately, a group of people, by calling in advance of a visit, may be able to arrange to see them by appointment.

❧ HENNA POT ❧

CONGREGATION EMANU-EL
1 East 65th Street
New York, NY 10021-6596
212-744-1400
Hours: Write to Reva Kirschberg, Director of the Museum, to arrange a guided tour.

Be forewarned: it takes planning to arrange a visit to this collection. It is usually available only to scholars, but, by appointment, visitors can see two cases of objects on display and, if possible, the sanctuary and ark. The reward is great, because the collection has outstanding examples of Judaica.

The building itself is fabulous. It was finished just a month before the stock market crash of October 1929. Enormous, handsome, and opulent, with Siena travertine marble on the vestibule walls and floors, it gave no hint of the coming economic debacle. There is seating for 2,500 people in the sanctuary.

Highlight: *One of the display cases contains a Moroccan wedding outfit: a jacket of thickly embroidered cotton in green, red, and yellow; a belt of woven red, orange, blue, wrapped metallic, and undyed cotton thread in complicated abstract patterns; and a crown of seed pearls, gold beads, and semiprecious stones of opalescent greens, blues, and pinks.*

The intriguing customs of such ceremonies are represented by a small, round, glazed bowl, painted in bright colors. This bowl was made to hold henna, which North African Jews put on the face and hands of a bride and other women in the bridal party. They believed henna was protection from evil.

◆ ORCHARD STREET ◆

THE LOWER EAST SIDE TENEMENT MUSEUM
97 Orchard Street
New York, NY 10002
212-431-0233
Hours: Tuesday through Friday, 11 to 4; Sunday, 10 to 3.

As many as 10,000 people lived at 97 Orchard Street, on the Lower East Side of New York City, from 1863 to 1935. The six-story, red brick building was, during those 72 years, the first home on American soil for many immigrants to the United States.

Today, 97 Orchard Street is a living museum. The new Ellis Island museum is, justifiably, drawing crowds, but that is just the beginning: the Lower East Side is where the immigrants went after they were processed at Ellis Island. They began their new life here, and if you want to know, to feel, to touch and smell what that life was like, 97 Orchard Street is the place to begin. On Sundays, the street is closed to traffic and sidewalk sales are in full swing. Peddlers with pushcarts join the other merchants who move their wares outdoors. The atmosphere of yesteryear is heightened by the presence of Orthodox Jews in their dark coats, black hats, and long beards. Katz's Delicatessen, perhaps the most famous deli in the world (midtown's Stage Delicatessen is championed by many deli mavens), sends out gusty whiffs of kosher pickles, corned beef, and pastrami.

A visit to the Tenement Museum is a haunting experience, especially for any child of pre-World War II immigrants. The apartments at

97 Orchard Street were condemned and closed to further rental when new building codes took effect in 1929; the last resident left in 1936. When they were discovered by the museum's curator, Anita Jacobson, in 1988, they were like a time capsule.

The Lower East Side Tenement Museum is not a sanitized, upbeat, romantic version of New World promises come true. As is true of many restorations, it would probably be cheaper to tear 97 Orchard Street down and rebuild it from scratch. But to lose it would be outrageous. The curators persist in moving slowly toward their goal of authenticity. I have to tell you that this museum is not finished.

When it is complete, there will be six apartments furnished as they might have been at various points during the building's history. For example, among the first wave of Lower East Side immigrants were pre–Civil War blacks who had bought their freedom. One of the families represented will be the Washingtons, a freed black couple, and their boarder, a runaway slave. There will be a Chinese immigrant and a German seamstress. As time goes on, the other tenants will become known. Actors will play the parts of these East Side immigrants.

Since the idea for this museum was conceived and the building's preserved condition was serendipitously discovered, genealogists and others have been tracing the names and backgrounds of its residents. They had not yet located any of the building's survivors, when, on December 15, 1988, an article in *The New York Times* described the beginnings and goals of the new museum.

About four weeks later, a letter to the editor appeared in the *Times*. A man named Max Mason described his family's arrival from Russia in 1921, his first impressions of 97 Orchard Street's tiny kitchen and wood-burning stove, and the teeming life of Orchard Street, which he watched from the fire escape. In the heat of summer, the fire escape became the children's "air conditioned" bedroom. He spoke no English when he arrived, and one day, coming home from school alone, he became completely and terrifyingly lost:

I knew I'd never see my mother and father again. And then I saw it! Way off in the distance there was a house with red fire escapes! And I remembered, when I left for school that morning, there were two men in white overalls, and they were painting our fire escapes red! I began to take aim for those fire escapes and my heart started pounding as I got nearer, street by street, and, sure enough, there was 97 Orchard Street, and I was home again. . . .

So far, the nation's first and only tenement museum has raised enough money to rent the ground-floor spaces and establish offices, galleries, and a theater. Although not yet fully operational, these facilities present an ongoing series of exhibits and dramatizations of New York history. Guided Sunday walks highlight different facets of the neighborhood life and history.

Highlight: *Museum members receive a newsletter, Tenement Times, that keeps them in touch with the museum's progress and research. In the first issue was a column devoted to "Soups from Tenement Kitchens," and recipes were included: Dee Dee Daily's West African Chicken Soup, Malachy McCormick's Irish Boiled Chicken and Broth, Rosa (Loh Mooi Kwei) Ross's Cantonese Chicken Soup, Hortense Kreukels' Bavarian Chicken Soup, and the broth that cured a million colds, Rebecca Arnowitz's Hungarian-Jewish Chicken Soup.*

❧ THE MOST ❧

THE JEWISH MUSEUM
Temporary quarters (through late 1992):
The New York Historical Society
Central Park West at 77th Street
Offices: 1865 Broadway, 4th floor
New York, NY 10023
212-399-3430 (information recording)
Hours: Sunday, Tuesday, Wednesday, Thursday, 10 to 5;
Friday, 10 to 3.
Permanent location (reopening date to be announced):
Fifth Avenue and 92nd Street

The Jewish Museum in New York is the largest and most important institution of its kind in the Western Hemisphere. In the collection are more than 14,000 works of art and artifacts covering 4,000 years of Jewish history.

The museum opened in 1904 as part of the Jewish Theological Seminary of America, in whose library it was first established. In 1947, the collection moved into a handsome, six-story mansion on

Fifth Avenue, the gift of Frieda Schiff Warburg. She was the daughter of railroad tycoon Jacob Schiff, whose heirs also donated over 300 turn-of-the-century paintings by James Jacques Tissot, illustrating the Hebrew bible. (Jacob Schiff, along with the Chancellor of the Seminary, Cyrus Adler, was a principal backer of Harvard University's Semitic Museum. See page 32.)

The design of the Warburg mansion, built in 1908, is French Gothic. The architect was C. P. H. Gilbert, one of the important names of his time, and the fashionable Gothic Revival had spread to America from England.

As the museum's collection grew and space got tighter, one inadequate and architecturally undistinguished 1962 addition was made to the building. More recently, a major change was decided upon, one that will literally double gallery space. The building addition, designed by Kevin Roche, is a more startling concept than almost any recent addition to a landmark building: instead of endeavoring to harmonize a new structural design with the existing building, the architect reproduced the building almost stone for stone, window for window, spire for spire. If Roche had attached a skyscraper to the upper floors, the rendering would scarcely have been less controversial. To some, the new structure destroys the integrity of the old, which was tall and narrow; the added girth of the expanded museum entirely changes the aesthetics of the building. To others, the design is the best possible solution, and—no small victory—the neighbors like it.

To accomplish the changes, The Jewish Museum closed its doors for approximately two years. The scheduled reopening at the end of 1992 will be accompanied by a new core exhibition on the Jewish experience as well as new classrooms and expanded gallery space for the permanent collection.

In this collection are works of historic, artistic, and religious significance; ethnographic material; archaeological artifacts and documentary photographs; ceremonial metalwork; textiles; numismatics; and paintings and sculpture. The broadcasting archives have programs such as a conversation with humorist Sam Levenson, Adolf Eichmann's testimony, and Edward R. Murrow's interview with David Ben-Gurion in 1956. Six thousand of the objects in the collection, from a 17th-century curtain for a Torah ark to a 20th-century self-portrait by the Russian artist Boris Schatz, were gathered and donated by Harry G. Friedman. Between 1941 and 1965, Friedman gave the Jewish Museum works he believed belonged in the public domain—ceremonial art, fine arts, and archaeological material.

Because the scope of this collection is so extraordinary, selecting just a few items to represent it is painful and even hazardous. One can only mention a few favorites, and one of mine is a photograph of the man who said:

The Jew could not preserve his treasures. . . . He has been practically always with a traveling bag on his shoulders and without knowing where he would have to go the very next day. Therefore any antiquities saved from the repeated catastrophes and diaspora are of the greatest value.

Hadji Ephraim Benguiat, who wrote these words in 1931, was grey-bearded and mustached. He was photographed wearing a turban, a long, wrinkled linen coat and robe, and a twisted, patterned silk cincture around his substantial middle. His feet were bare. His most outstanding feature, even more than his direct, inquisitive look, is the warm smile beneath his frizzy beard.

Benguiat was born in Izmir, Turkey, the son and grandson of dealers in antiquity. He too became a collector. He had passion, vision, and variety in his collection, which was one of the earliest to come to the Jewish Museum in New York City. In Benguiat's collection there is, in ink and watercolor, a text from Ecclesiastes in "micrography," minute writing. The text is shaped into a sphere representing an astrolabe, the instrument used to measure the sun's altitude. From the Benguiat family has come a nearly nine-foot-wide piece of furniture that resembles an enormous Renaissance sideboard with scroll-like designs and pilasters embellished with gilt. It is, in fact, a Torah ark, dated 1533, from Urbino, Italy. A poem in Hebrew lettering, painted on the cabinet doors, is broadly based on the Scriptures but takes some poetic license with the word ark, to suit the poet's rhyme scheme.

Another favorite piece, in the folk art collection, is a 1910 walrus tusk engraved with portraits of a top-hatted, bearded man and a sternly coiffed woman, and a Hebrew inscription wishing the recipient a Happy New Year from Nome, Alaska. An Alaskan Eskimo nicknamed Happy Jack was the artist. Quite irresistible, too, is a

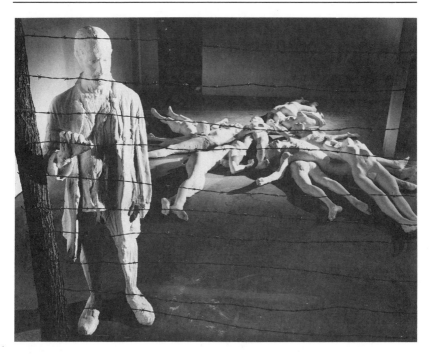

The Holocaust by George Segal, 1982. Courtesy of The Jewish Museum, New York.

Hanukkah lamp made, in 1974, by Mae Shafter Rockland: on a two-tiered base covered with stars and stripes are eight plastic figures of the Statue of Liberty with holders for Hanukkah candles held in her torch-bearing right hand.

Besides the richness of its own collection, over the years this museum has originated and hosted a large number of fabulously diverse and provocative temporary exhibitions. For example, From Seder to Stella: The Art of Passover in the Collections of the Jewish Museum; Robert Capa: Photographs from Israel, 1948–1950; Golem! Danger, Deliverance and Art; and A People in Print: Jewish Journalism in America.

Highlight: *A Torah ark from any time and place usually resembles the contemporary decorative arts of its place of origin. One ark from 18th-century Bavaria is, however, incomparable. The false marble front of the cabinet—a painted trompe l'oeil—is one distinction; the*

Arab Fisherman by Reuven Rubin, 1928. Courtesy of The Jewish Museum, New York.

Hanukkah lamp. Italy, 17th century. Courtesy of The Jewish Museum, New York.

scrollwork, symbolic plant, and crown are another. But the two loony lions on the top of the piece have no equal. They don't look a bit like real lions—they don't have tails or manes—and they seem quite naked. Still, they stand heraldically atop the ark, holding a sequined Torah crown, and wearing expressions meant to be ferocious. Their sharp fangs rise from their lower jaws! Could Dracula have been modeled after this charming couple, or were they modeled after him?

◆ LIBERTY AND MORE ◆

ELLIS ISLAND IMMIGRATION MUSEUM AND THE STATUE OF LIBERTY NATIONAL MONUMENT
Ellis Island/Liberty Island, NY 10004
212-363-3200
Hours: 212-269-5755, for exact times of ferry departures and return trips. Ferries depart from Liberty State Park (Jersey City, NJ) and Battery Park (Lower Manhattan). Passengers may disembark at either the Statue of Liberty or Ellis Island.

THE NEW COLOSSUS

. . . Here at our sea-washed, sunset gates shall stand
A mighty woman with a torch, whose flame
Is the imprisoned lightning, and her name
Mother of Exiles. From her beacon-hand
Glows world-wide welcome; . . .
. . . Give me your tired, your poor,
Your huddled masses yearning to breathe free.
The wretched refuse of your teeming shore.
Send these, the homeless, tempest-tost to me,
I lift my lamp beside the golden door!

Emma Lazarus was an American poet and a pioneer Zionist. Her famous poem, inspired by the plight of European Jewry, was inscribed on a tablet at the base of the Statue of Liberty. Today, the tablet is inside the base, in a museum devoted to the "mother of exiles." This museum is often overlooked by the hordes of visitors who now make their way to Ellis Island and miss the fascinating story of the Statue's history.

At the entrance to the museum, a full-scale replica of Liberty's face closes the normal distance between viewers and the top of the Statue and conveys its true dimensions. The face is eight and one-half feet high, the nose, four and one-half feet high, the mouth, three feet high, and each eye, two and one-half feet across. A copy of the Statue's left foot, and the original plaster model for her left ear, brought from Auguste Bartholdi's studio, are also on display.

Bartholdi also sculpted a bust of the French historian, Edouard de Laboulaye, the man who had proposed that his government present the United States, upon its 100th anniversary, with an important gift that would commemorate the French-American alliance during the American Revolution. Bartholdi's original bust of Laboulaye is in the museum.

It is always fascinating to track the sources of an artist's inspiration, and there is a display that shows the diverse images that influenced Bartholdi, including Roman coins and, tradition says, his mother's face. The wood and lead molds, a plaster model, the actual tools used in the Statue's fabrication, and a video program describing the copper-crafting technique required for the Statue's construction and restoration are worth visiting. A three-dimensional, cut-away model, over eight feet high, allows the technically inclined an even better idea of how the pieces went together and particularly how Liberty withstands the windy gusts blowing across New York harbor.

The Statue of Liberty's fame would be dazzling under any circumstances, but, considering the commercialization of her image, the dimensions of her notoriety are mind-boggling. There is a line of miniature statues that seems to reach infinity, and there are items of folk art, posters, advertisements, travel posters, political cartoons, World War I Liberty Bond posters, sheet music covers, and multitudes of other reproductions. A tour is fun for Liberty lovers.

The museum is also a good place to pick up some winning trivia. For example:

- The land on which Liberty stands was originally called Bedloe's Island. It was renamed Liberty Island in 1956.
- Liberty arrived in New York harbor in more than 200 crates, in 1885.

Both curious and apprehensive, immigrants waited anxiously to be processed into America. This Hungarian family arriving at Ellis Island around 1910 was photographed by Augustus F. Sherman, registry room chief clerk of Ellis Island from 1897 to 1924. Courtesy of National Park Service.

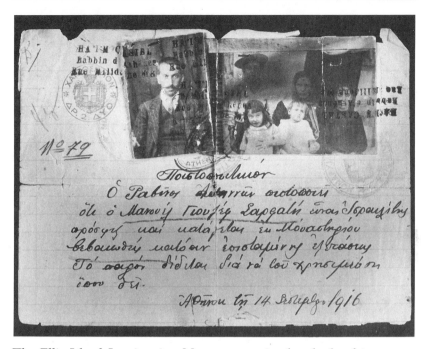

The Ellis Island Immigration Museum contains hundreds of important historical artifacts like this 1916 Greek passport. Courtesy of MetaForm.

- A one-quarter scale copy of the Statue of Liberty was given to France by the United States in 1885. It was first erected on the Square of the United States in Paris, and was later moved to the Bridge of Grenelle, over the River Seine, where it still stands.
- Dedication ceremonies were held on October 28, 1886, with President Grover Cleveland in attendance.
- Emma Lazarus's poem was placed on a tablet affixed to the pedestal of the statue in 1903.
- Bartholdi died in France at the age of 70, in 1904. There is a museum dedicated to him in Colmar, France.

Highlight: *Don't miss the five-foot-long wrench, made in France, that was used to tighten the bolts that anchor the statue to the pedestal.*

This dormitory room in the Main Building has been restored as part of The Ellis Island Immigration Museum. Courtesy Peter B. Kaplan.

⊛ THE GOLDEN DOOR ⊛

I cannot begin to tell you how beautiful it was when I went to Ellis Island. Although it was early December, it was as warm as a spring day, the city was silvered by the sunlight, the water sparkled, and the sky was bluer than Jack Benny's eyes.

I had imagined the immigration building many times, but it was the inside I thought about. On that sunny day, my first impression was the same as that of the boatloads of immigrants who were brought there, particularly during the decades between 1897 and 1924, when the greatest waves of would-be newcomers arrived. The brick and stone facade, the copper roof, arched windows, huge doors, and towers have a bold, powerful, palatial if not imperialistic look. The Beaux Arts building, painstakingly restored at a cost of $160 million, must have reminded many newcomers,

Millions of immigrants passed through the dramatic and vast Great Hall in the Main Building at Ellis Island. It has been restored to the way it looked in 1918.

perhaps regretfully, of the countries from which they were seeking refuge.

As I entered the huge hall, I envisioned it peopled by the tired, shabbily dressed refugees. Wealthier immigrants were not required to pass through Ellis Island. The transatlantic steamers were brought to anchor at quarantine areas, and immigration officials boarded to give these new arrivals the necessary processing on shipboard. The rest of the passengers were dispatched on barges or deposited on receiving piers upstream in the Hudson, to await ferries to Ellis Island.

When my uncle arrived in 1905 with his mother, sister, and brother, the health inspector marked his coat with chalk because he seemed to have an eye problem. My grandmother, according to family history, secretly rubbed the mark off and got her small brood into the New World intact. That is only one of 17 million Ellis Island stories, but I thought of it as I roamed the rooms where newcomers had moved from medical exams to legal exams. They climbed the enormous flights of stairs to the Great Hall, past doctors stationed at the landings to pick out anyone who might be limping, breathing too heavily, or otherwise disabled. At the top, each immigrant had to walk in a circle around a doctor who looked for any sign of contagious disease or other problems. If any were found, the person's clothing was marked with chalk: L for lameness, H for suspected heart disease, and E for eye problems.

The next test was a series of questions: "What is your name?" "Do you have any relatives here?" "Where are you going?" "Are you an anarchist?" "Are you a polygamist?" The wrong answer brought another symbol, SI, signifying a required appearance before the Board of Special Inquiry. Eighty percent of the immigrants stayed on Ellis Island three to five hours—about as long as a visitor today will need to tour the museum. Twenty percent were detained for a longer time, and about two percent were denied admission.

No matter how trite it may sound, the halls and corridors of the Ellis Island building seem to echo with ghosts, and not all of them immigrant arrivals in the late 19th century. Archaeologists who participated in Ellis Island's restoration found layer upon layer of fascinating information.

Gull Island to Native Americans, Dyre's or Bucking Island in the late 17th and early 18th century, and Gibbet (because of hangings of traitors and pirates there) or Anderson's Island in the pre-Revolutionary period, this three-acre mud flat served as a landing for oystermen and shad fishermen and as a military installation. But the archaeologists' big surprise was in discovering evidence of its prehistoric culture—pottery fragments and flint implements from the period between 1000 B.C.E. to 1600 A.C.E.

The first documented building on the island was a tavern constructed around 1750. The man who owned it by the end of the 18th century was Samuel Ellis, a merchant who rented boats, rakes, and nets, sold shad and herring by the barrel, and provided a place for New Yorkers to party off shore. The island took on his name.

The state acquired the southeastern part of the island and built Fort Gibson there, to shore up its harbor defenses against the English and French in case of attack. The tavern still flourished, however. By 1890 the processing of immigrants to the United States had become such an enormous task that the federal government took it over from the states and Ellis Island was chosen as the site for the entry procedure. The first immigrant station was built in 1892 but was destroyed by fire in 1897. The main building, now the museum, replaced it in 1900. The peak of immigration occurred in 1907, then gradually declined. During 1914 and 1915, homeless men were brought over from Manhattan at night and taken back in the morning. During the two World Wars, prisoners and suspect aliens were imprisoned on the island.

The restoration, and in some instances the redesign, of the 220,000-square-foot building was a challenging project, undertaken by architects of New York City and Boston. The year chosen to represent was 1918. Two of the most publicized new features are the canopy leading up to the building—a metal and glass structure reminiscent of scaffolding (the original awning was of cloth)—and a replacement of the vanished stairway described above.

The exhibits are excellent. A statistical analysis of Ellis Island's immigration patterns, brought vividly to life through a series of graphic inventions, is unexpectedly fascinating. The Dormitory Room looks like multiples of sleeping accommodations in a submarine. The exhibit called Treasures from Home—objects immigrants brought with them—is a fascinating potpourri of memorabilia.

◄ UPTOWN ►

YESHIVA UNIVERSITY MUSEUM
2520 Amsterdam Avenue
New York, NY 10033
212-960-5390
Hours: Tuesday, Wednesday, Thursday, 10:30 to 5; Sunday, 12 to 6.

Shortly after it was founded in 1973, the Yeshiva University Museum commissioned ten scale models for its first exhibit on the history of synagogues. The project required special ingenuity: the 3rd-century Dura Europos model, for instance, was based on plans projected from archaeological digs and photos. Other models depended on reconstructions of lost or damaged buildings.

The model of Tempio Israelitico in Florence is stunning. From 1864 to 1870, Florence enjoyed its glory as capital of Italy, and Jews who lived there had just recently acquired status as full citizens. They felt both pride and patriotism. Three architects, one of whom was Jewish, designed their house of worship in the early 1870s and it was dedicated in 1882, an extravaganza of rose granite and tan travertine marble, elaborate and ornamented arched windows, turrets, and copper onion domes. The Islamic style, used in many European synagogues, is vivid here, particularly in the exotic, richly colored, mosquelike interior, masterfully reproduced in the model.

The Florentine building is an amazing contrast to the synagogue of Zabludow, Poland; one would believe that entirely different religions were practiced in the two places. The Polish model is of a wooden building with a series of overlapping shingle roofs that both peak and curve. It has board siding, a balcony with rails, and small windows. The Florentine synagogue was damaged during World War II and again by the flood of 1966, but is still standing. The 17th-century Polish gem was utterly destroyed during the war, which makes Yeshiva's model all the more a treasure. The museum provides a marvelous opportunity to see the various styles of synagogue architecture—from Zabludow, Poland to Newport, Rhode Island (Yeshiva has a model of Touro; see page 113). Usually, six of the ten models are on display somewhere in the building.

Architecture is just a small part of this major collection, which has grown impressively in a fairly short time and includes fine art, folk art, Judaica, and books. Temporary exhibitions are varied, drawing from museums all over the world as well as from Yeshiva's own collection. The Jewish Wedding and Daily Life in Ancient Israel are examples of two themes that have recently been explored.

An exhibition I visited was called The Sephardic Journey, 1492–1992, a chronicle of the settlement of Spanish and Portuguese Jews after their 15th-century expulsion by Spain. The exhibit was scheduled to remain through 1992.

The rich intellectual and artistic life of the dispersed Sephardim is portrayed through paintings, Judaica, manuscripts, and costumes. It took four years from conception to realization of this exhibit; many of the objects borrowed for the show had never left their countries of origin. From Augsburg, Germany, came an enormous 17th-century silvered brass basin with a repouse, or raised-relief scene of the Queen of Sheba presenting gifts to King Solomon. The basin, used by rabbis to wash their hands during a ceremony, was part of a dioramalike display portraying a wedding of that era. A wedding dress from the museum's own significant costume collection is the stuff of fantasies: a burgundy velvet, 19th-century Moroccan robe, elaborately embroidered with gold-washed silver threads. Traditionally, before the ceremony, people came to look at the wedding gown and the rest of the trousseau and dowry, which were put on display for their viewing.

The Yeshiva Museum is devotedly educational. A constant stream of excited children enjoys tours spiced with stories and puppet shows. The museum is interdisciplinary and endeavors to give a context to objects on view.

The major gallery for changing exhibitions is on the fourth floor of the building, and rare manuscripts from the university archives often complement the theme of an exhibit.

On the ground floor, the expansive galleries often have contemporary art exhibits as well as various important pieces from the museum's permanent collection, such as the Trent Manuscript. This manuscript is a 15th-century documentation of the accusation and trial of the Jews of Trent (now Trento, Italy), who were blamed for the ritual murder of a two-year-old Christian boy. According to Christian lore, Jews used the blood of their victim to make the Passover matzos. Such strange accusations, reminiscent of the Salem witch trials, flared up frequently in Europe, starting in the 12th century. Usually, as in Trent, Jews were murdered or banished in the aftermath. The related manuscripts reveal the strange, obsessive nature of anti-Semitism during the medieval period, and the remarkable handwritten and illuminated book in Yeshiva's collection is a rare acquisition.

Unique in a quite different but related mode are two other historic documents. One, sent from Monticello, in Virginia, on May 28, 1818, begins:

I thank you for the Discourse on the consecration of the Synagogue in your city, with which you have been pleased to favor me. I have read it with pleasure and instruction, having learnt from it some valuable facts in Jewish history which I did not know before. Your sect by its sufferings has furnished a remarkable proof of the universal spirit of religious intolerance, inherent in every sect, disclaimed by all while feeble, and practiced by all when in power. . . . I salute you with great respect and esteem. [signed] Th. Jefferson.

The recipient was Mordecai Manuel Noah.

The other document is a record book of the affairs of the earliest American synagogue, founded by the first Jews who landed in New

Trial of the Jews of Trent. Trent, Italy, ca. 1478. Courtesy of Yeshiva University Museum, New York.

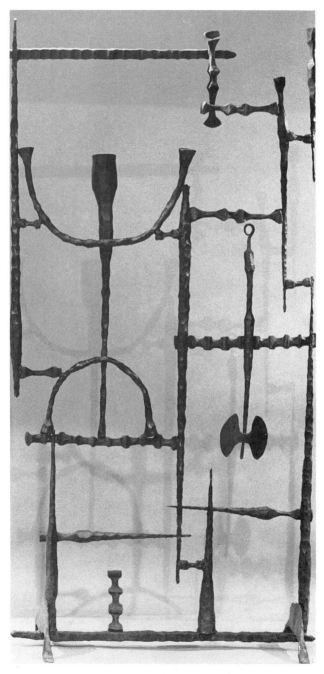

The Gate by David Palombo (1920–1966). Gift of Mr. and Mrs. Selig Burrows. Courtesy of Yeshiva University Museum, New York.

Ottoman Jewish bridal costume, Ottoman Empire, 19th century. Courtesy
of Yeshiva University Museum, New York.

The Bride by Abraham Rattner (1892–1978). Gift of Mr. and Mrs. Selig Burrows. Courtesy of Yeshiva University Museum, New York.

York, in 1654. Accounts were kept assiduously, except for a period when it was noted that the register of those present could not be taken because of the interruption of the Revolutionary War.

A brightly colored oil painting on a gallery wall, *The Bride*, by American expressionist Abraham Rattner, has a story attached to it. Randi Glickberg, the museum's administrator, went to pick up *The Bride* from the donors, a family who live on Long Island. While Glickberg was there, she commented on a handsome wrought-iron sculpture. Its donor offered to give the sculpture to the museum, too. Although Glickberg did not realize it at the time, she had succeeded in bringing another important piece of art to Yeshiva. The piece was by a well-known Israeli sculptor, David Palombo, who also made gates for the Knesset in Jerusalem.

The number and variety of discoveries at the Yeshiva Museum are great—samplers, wimples, purim plates, photographs, and paper-cuts. One papercut from 1900 has a lion and a stag guarding a Torah ark and carries the Hebrew inscription: "I will lift up mine eyes unto the mountains. . . ."

A photograph used by the museum in an exhibition called Ashkenz: The German Jewish Heritage is reproduced on a postcard. A little girl, about a year old and wearing a white dress with puffy sleeves, is sitting in a large wooden chair that has long, curved handles and big wheels—a primitive sort of perambulator. A second child, three or four years old, with long curls showing from under her hat, is holding the curved handles. She is dressed in a fine coat, high button shoes, and a muff. The children are posed in front of a painted woodland landscape and have beautifully sweet, innocent faces. The picture was taken in 1908 at Frankfurt-am-Main, Germany.

❧ YIDISHER VISENSHAFTLIKHER INSTITUT ❧

YIVO INSTITUTE FOR JEWISH RESEARCH
1048 Fifth Avenue
New York, NY 10028
212-535-6700
Hours: Monday through Friday, 9:30 to 5:30.

Vilna, once its capital, was called the Jerusalem of Lithuania. Beginning in the early 17th century, it was a prominent center for rabbinic studies. In the 19th century, it was the center for the Jewish Enlightenment, socialism, and Zionism. The Jewish population, once 140,000, had dropped to about 80,000 by the early 1900s and was a mere 16,000 in 1970. One of the world's most disturbing photographs was taken, in 1941, of the Jews of Vilna digging their own graves.

YIVO (Yidisher Visenshaftlikher Institut) was founded in Vilna in 1925 as a cultural resource to support scholars in the humanities and social sciences who were researching Jewish life. The original headquarters of YIVO was destroyed by the Nazis in 1942, although half of YIVO's documents had been moved to New York in 1940. The other half were presumed lost, until just recently. In the summer of 1989, YIVO's executive director, Samuel Norich, was doing research in a library in Lithuania and was given four packets wrapped in paper and tied with strings. He discovered that more than 40,000 pages of archival material had been saved— accounts of the Ukrainian pogrom of 1919, autobiographies of young people of Eastern Europe who had responded to a writing contest for Jewish teenagers in 1932, and letters.

"I can't even describe the feeling of holding in my hands letters written by Max Weinreich which nobody had seen or touched in 50 years," said Norich. Weinreich was a renowned Yiddish writer and one of YIVO's founders. How this material escaped Nazi destruction is still uncertain, and Norich is hopeful that the documents will eventually come to New York as part of YIVO's archives, which contain over 22 million items and are one of the major collections of Yiddish material in the world.

The flavor of Yiddish life can be seen on paper, microfilm, tapes and video discs. There are also posters, playbills, music, folklore, maps, art, newspaper clippings. Major fields of specialization are the Jewish history of Eastern Europe from the 17th century through 1939; the Holocaust and its aftermath; the immigration, settlement, and social history of the Jews in the United States; and Jewish education and culture.

All of these are housed in an oddly anomalous setting, an elegant mansion on Fifth Avenue. The cluttered archives office, full of metal file cabinets, desks, and computers, is in a room with a marble fireplace, an enormous crystal chandelier, and marble and wood paneling. The latter is painted grey and detailed with gold—a baroque and ornamental background for the room's activities.

The sense of paradox grew stronger as I sat before a video display terminal in this room, looking at photographs from turn-of-the-century Odessa and the pre-World War II years. A studio portrait showed three sisters wearing wide hats and dressed in the "height of fashion"; another photo was of five bookbinders wearing high collars and gazing intensely at the camera. I found a view of bustling streets, streetcars, and an ornate, round opera house; a group of women in white dresses and head coverings, who were working in a kitchen, preparing meals for the needy; and a dreadful series of photographs showing victims of the 1905 pogroms.

Thousands of photos are on this laser-read videodisc, which was developed for a Jewish Museum (page 66) exhibition. The public is welcome to look through the photos, but anyone who wishes to do so should call to make advance arrangements.

The videodisc room is on the second floor, which is reached by an elegant, curving staircase; at the top, exhibitions of works of art from the archives are often available. When I visited, this space was filled with a collection of sketches by an immigrant to America who went back to Europe between the two World Wars.

Downstairs, to the right of the front entrance, is a gallery for temporary exhibitions. Using material from its own collection, YIVO had put together a show on Shalom Aleichem, the "Jewish Mark Twain," who was born in the Ukraine in 1859, lived for many years in Kiev, and came to the United States at the turn of the century. His work was revived and reached a wide audience via "Fiddler on the Roof," but his fame was never less than extraordinary among the Jewish population.

On one of the display panels was a map that showed the route of Shalom Aleichem's funeral procession in 1916. It started from 116th Street and went all the way to a cemetery in Brooklyn. One hundred and fifty thousand people lined the streets to pay their last respects! It was the largest funeral cortege in New York history to that date. Shalom Aleichem's burial was said to have laid to rest, symbolically, the Old World generation he represented. The inscription on his gravestone, which he wrote, is translated on page 31.

Highlight: *To the left of the stairwell in the entrance hall was an odd apparition, a Victorian oak case with a glass front, containing what I first thought to be shrunken heads. Not quite. On close inspection they turned out to be small wax models — the dusty, grisly, humorous faces of* *characters from a play put on by Yiddish actor and producer Maurice Schwartz in 1933.*

❧ ASHKENAZI ❧

LEO BAECK INSTITUTE
129 East 73rd Street
New York, NY 10021
212-744-6400
Hours: Monday through Friday, 9 to 4:45; Friday during winter, 9 to 3.

Over time, the term Ashkenazi has generally come to mean the tradition and culture of most European Jews with German backgrounds, as opposed to those with Spanish and Portuguese—Sephardic—heritage. Like many such definitions, origins are hazy and applications are fluid. Ashkenazi at first referred only to Germany and occurred quite frequently in rabbinic literature dating back to the 12th century. Today, its meaning is often stretched to include all the Jews of Eastern and Western Europe. The Leo Baeck Institute is limited to German-speaking Jewry—a population nearly wiped out by the Nazis.

The earliest reliable written report of Jewish settlements in the Rhineland came via a decree of Emperor Constantine the Great, who commanded the Jews to participate in the maintenance and defense of the city of Cologne. The decree was in 331, and it does not tell us how long the Jewish people had been living there. A legend says that thousands of members of the Biblical tribe of Benjamin fled a massacre in the ancient town of Gibeah, in Israel, and settled in Worms, but there is no confirming evidence.

During the Middle Ages, from around 900 to 1500, Jews of the Rhineland were persecuted but they were also able to pursue the learning they so loved and to build intellectual and artistic achievements and institutions. In later centuries, this region produced Moses Mendelssohn, Karl Marx, Sigmund Freud, Franz Kafka, and Martin Buber. Photos of important Ashkenazis of more recent years decorate the curving wall of a stairwell at the Institute; they include 24 German Nobel prizewinners, including Paul Erlich (Medicine, 1908), Alfred Fried (Peace, 1911), Albert Einstein (Physics, 1921), Nelly Sachs (Literature, 1966), and Henry Kissinger (Peace, 1973).

Leo Baeck was born in Berlin, where he became a rabbi and the spiritual leader of German Reform Jewry. He was sent to Terezin in 1943, but he survived the war. Afterward, he settled in London and headed the World Union for Progressive Judaism.

New York's Leo Baeck Institute (there are others in Jerusalem and London) is in a lovely townhouse that was built at the turn of the century. Founded in 1955, the Institute has a library, archives, and an art collection, all of which are drawn upon for exhibitions. In the art collection are 90 paintings, 3,000 drawings, watercolors, and prints, and several sculptures. Impressionist Lesser Ury, who has been called a tragic figure and a poet of moods, is represented, as is Max Liebermann, the greatest German painter of the late 19th century.

Changing exhibitions are usually drawn from the Institute's own collection, although, when I was there, many items had been borrowed for an exhibit about Austro-Hungarian Jewish soldiers from 1788 until the end of the Hapsburg Empire in 1918. Uniforms, a beautifully illuminated manuscript, and military memorabilia underlined the loyalty that Jews had for the Hapsburg dynasty, which they idealized as their protector against anti-Semitic attacks.

Highlight: *Take a good look at the facade of this five-story townhouse. Each level is treated differently. The decoratively framed doorway is flanked by two quite small windows; the second story is embellished with columns and three tall, arched windows; a lion's head and shield ornaments the wall between the third and fourth floor, and two heraldic bas relief sculptures sit beneath the tiled roof.*

⇜ LIBRARY LIONS ∾

NEW YORK PUBLIC LIBRARY
Jewish Division
Central Research Library, Room 84
Fifth Avenue at 42nd Street
New York, NY 10018-2788
212-930-0601
Hours: Tuesday, 11 to 7:30; Wednesday, 11 to 6; Thursday, 11 to 6;
Friday and Saturday, 10 to 6.

Every year, nearly 10,000 people—college students, authors, clergy, professors, elderly immigrants and their young grandchildren—take advantage of the unparalleled resources of the Jewish Division of the New York Public Library. Newspapers and periodicals printed in Europe and America over the past two centuries, written in German, Polish, Russian, Hungarian, and Czech, are a typical example. Visitors gain insight into the day-to-day cultural, religious, and social life in a multitude of Jewish communities that are now vanished. Among other publications are those produced for the immigrants who arrived on these shores, documenting the conditions they faced in American cities.

The library offers a comprehensive and balanced chronicle of the religious and secular history of the Jews through its 250,000 books, microforms, manuscripts, newspapers, periodicals, and ephemera from everywhere. One of the great collections of Judaica in the world, accessible for both scholarly and personal use, can be found on the ground floor of the library in room 84.

Among the rare books and periodicals (40 are from the 15th century and over 1,500 are from the 16th century) is the title page of Perush ha-Torah. The original work was a commentary on the Pentateuch by Moses Nahmanides (1194–1270), a Spanish rabbi, Talmudist, philosopher, cabalist, and poet, and an influential and controversial member of his community. The page in the library's collection was in the first book printed in the city of Lisbon, in 1489. The ornamental border is delicately inscribed with minute details of flower and animal forms entwined with vines.

The Jewish Division was founded in 1897 with a gift from Jacob Schiff, the renowned financier and philanthropist who was, in many ways, the unofficial lay spokesperson for American Jews. He played an

A late 14th-century German illuminated mahzor (prayer book) depicting the Gates of Mercy with a prayer usually spoken at the close of the Yom Kippur service. Courtesy of The Jewish Division, The New York Public Library.

important role in many institutions, including Yeshiva College, the Jewish Theological Seminary, Hebrew Union College, the Jewish Publication Society, and the American Jewish Committee. His daughter, Dorothy Schiff, was equally well-known in later years as the publisher and editor-in-chief of *The New York Post*.

In 1989, the Jewish Division quarters in a Beaux Arts reading room were renovated. A new reference desk and a special reading room for rare books were added. The wood-paneled walls were refinished; tables, chairs, and lighting were all improved; and new bookcases were provided for the 800-volume catalog.

Highlight: *Probably the most famous lions in America, next to Bert Lahr and MGM's Leo, are the two huge beasts at the entrance to the New York Public Library. Considering the collection just described, it is tempting to think of these alert stone guardians as stand-ins for the Lion of Judah.*

◄ TO EDUCATE ►

ROCKLAND CENTER FOR HOLOCAUST STUDIES
17 South Madison Avenue
Spring Valley, NY 10977
914-356-2700
Hours: Sunday through Thursday, 12 to 4.

A permanent exhibit on the Holocaust includes four videos. In addition to artifacts and memorabilia, there are original art works, taped interviews of survivors, photos, and other educational material.

PENNSYLVANIA

❧ SERENDIPITY, ETC. ❧

THE TEMPLE JUDEA MUSEUM OF KENESETH ISRAEL
York Road and Township Line
Elkins Park, PA 19117
215-887-8700
Hours: Monday through Wednesday, 1 to 4; Friday evening, before and after Sabbath services; group tours by appointment.

Barbara Forman could hardly believe her luck: while doing research at the Civil War Library and Museum in Philadelphia, she asked the director whether he knew the whereabouts of Dr. Jacob da Silva Solis-Cohen's 1854 diploma from Central High School. Not only was the diploma quickly retrieved, but so were the good doctor's medical school diploma and license to practice medicine. Better yet, because the Civil War museum collects only military artifacts, Forman was given the documents, for the collection of The Temple Judea Museum of Keneseth Israel.

Dr. da Silva Solis-Cohen was an eminent Philadelphia physician who served in both the Union Army and Navy during the Civil War. The unexpected acquisition of his diplomas is an example of curatorial luck, the sort of small victory a museum visitor rarely learns about. The exhibit Barbara Forman was curating at the time was Keneseth Israel Families and the Civil War: Nine Vignettes in Blue and Gray. The vignettes are identified with nine members of the congregation who had fought during the war. Besides Dr. da Silva Solis-Cohen there were, for example, two 15-year-olds, Solomon Aarons and Isaac Snellenburg, who were footsoldiers in the Peninsula Campaign to take Richmond. Both fought in the fierce battle of Fair Oaks Swamp during which, on June 30, 1862, Snellenburg was killed. He was buried on the battlefield.

Aarons, a drummer boy, survived the battle and the war. According to military lore, his troops' green battle flag brought luck to Aarons and his regiment. The flag was given to the Independence Hall Museum in 1865. Unfortunately, after being displayed in the statehouse rotunda for 75 years, the fabric disintegrated. Instead of the flag, the curator was presented with a reproduction of a pen-and-ink sketch of the battle, done at the peak of the conflict, on the day Isaac Snellenberg was killed. In the background, clearly visible, is the lucky flag that protected young Aarons and his fighting companions.

The Civil War exhibit was presented for three months during the spring of 1987 in the Temple museum's gallery, in the synagogue. This museum's lively and diverse calendar usually offers three exhibits each year. These have included a retrospective of the silver, gold, wood, ivory, porcelain, and enameled ceremonial objects created by Daniel Blumberg, a Philadelphia dentist. They testify to an admirable manual dexterity, manifested, no doubt, in his profession as well as his pastime.

A exhibit called Ancient Israel: 3500 Years of Housewares and History used 41 everyday objects plus photos, maps, and a miniature model of an Israelite house to illustrate daily life of ages past. These humble objects are so evocative as to be nearly mystical. A five-inch-high, two-handled iron cooking pot, for instance, dates from about 800 to 586 B.C.E.; a small crack runs down an inch or two from the rim. How many ancient meals were prepared in this, and what were the ingredients? What were the topics of family conversation during the meals? Question leads to question, stirring the imagination.

Keneseth Israel's museum was opened in 1986. About 600 pieces represent the combined Judaica collections of two merged synagogues of suburban Philadelphia—ceremonial objects, paintings, etchings, fabrics, documents, and texts. A corps of 18 volunteers has taken a 20-week course, in order to project the museum's expertise when they give slide lectures and tours. Temporary exhibits change three times during the year.

When there are no temporary exhibits, the museum's own substantial and important collection is displayed. Among the paintings is one by Chaim Goldberg, who now lives and works in Houston, Texas. He was born in the ghetto of Kazimierz, Poland, on March 20, 1917, and studied at the High School of Fine Art in Krakow, the Academy of Fine Art in Warsaw, and the École des Beaux Arts in Paris.

After World War II, Goldberg went back to Poland and painted the ruins of the ghetto. These canvases are now in an Israeli museum. Later, he painted his home from memory and that remembered vision, also an oil painting, is in the Keneseth Israel collection. A figure is walking through the shtetl, apparently on his way to work. In the right-hand corner is Goldberg's family home; an upper window was in the upstairs room in which he painted as a young man. A small vegetable patch that his mother tended is visible, and, high on the hill in the background, stands the summer home of a king who ruled during the 14th century.

When Goldberg visited Keneseth Israel, he told the museum's curator, Judith Maslin, and its director, Dorothy Freedman, about his town. Jews had lived well there; they had been integrated into its economic and cultural life for 600 years. That life came to an end in 1942, when residents of the shtetl were all shipped to a concentration camp.

Highlight: *The oldest piece in the collection is a Torah Commentary from Italy, dated 1574. From Lancaster, Pennsylvania, has come the second oldest American ketubah, to the best of anyone's knowledge.*

❧ REALLY, REALLY BIG ❧

LEHIGH VALLEY REGION (including Allentown)
Monumental Sculpture
For a map, contact:
Department of Parks and Recreation
2700 Parkway Boulevard
Allentown, PA 18104
215-437-7628
Lehigh University
Bethlehem, PA 18015
215-758-3615 (information)

One man, Philip Berman, has made this region unique. What he has done doesn't fit into any conventional guidebook category, but then the most interesting things in life never do fit into categories.

Philip Berman was born just before World War I on a farm in Pennsburg, Pennsylvania. He was a student at Ursinus College when the opportunity came to launch a new business. He dropped out of school and started an International Harvester heavy truck dealership. He expanded into transporting beer, coast to coast, after Prohibition ended.

His career in trucking advanced. He married Muriel Mallin, an optometrist. World War II was spent in the Marine Corps as a gunner.

By the 1950s, Berman had made his first fortune. He had also moved to Allentown, the big city about 20 miles from Pennsburg. Instead of dabbling in politics as so many wealthy people do ("I hate politics," he told a reporter), Berman dove into public service. Thanks to him, Allentown's downtown was revitalized and a state system of public television was launched.

Muriel and Philip Berman also began collecting art. As they collected, they educated themselves, they became acquainted with artists, and they developed a taste for modern art.

In 1968, Berman bought Hess's department store. By the time he sold that business, about 10 years later, it had developed into more than 20 Hess stores. Most of the stores were enhanced by the installation of monumental contemporary sculptures in front of the building—that is, enhanced as far as the Bermans were concerned. Some local critics didn't like "those things" at all. The controversy seemed to energize Philip Berman.

The Bermans' philanthropy has been vast. From Israel to Allentown, they have donated more works of art than can be counted. Sculptures have been placed on all of the 14 state university campuses. Over 46 pieces are in Allentown alone (including *Wailing Walls*, an enormous work by Richard Gottleib at Union Terrace Park). There are numerous pieces on the nearby campuses of Cedar Crest College and Lehigh University. For example, *The Sacrifice of Isaac*, by Menashe Kadishman, rises from a bluff on Lehigh's Mountaintop Campus.

Most of the works the Bermans have donated are nonrepresentational. A great many are by Israeli artists—among them, Igael Tumarkin, a Holocaust survivor, whose works are both in the city and on the Lehigh campus.

Whatever their titles—*Variations of Mita Meshuna* (Tumarkin), *Flame* (John Reik) or *Untitled* (Dick Caswell)—all the works are provocative. Berman has repeated many times: "Art should elicit a response. . . . If people are indifferent, art has failed."

Highlight: *Ursinus College, from which Philip Berman dropped out to make his fortune, is in Collegeville, Pennsylvania, about an hour from Allentown. It has been a beneficiary of the Berman generosity in both sculptures (The Temple, by Mary Ann Unger, is there) and works on canvas and paper.*

In 1989, the college opened the Philip and Muriel Berman Museum of Art. Among the works in the collection is a very large Chagall, Lovers on a Bench. During the week of the opening celebrations, it was announced that the Allentown philanthropist had been named chairman of the board of directors of the Philadelphia Museum of Art. Breaking convention, which has been Philip Berman's custom, he was the first Jew ever named to the position.

MILITARY MEMORABILIA

HOLOCAUST AWARENESS MUSEUM OF DELAWARE VALLEY
Gratz College
Old York Road and Melrose Avenue
Melrose Park, PA 19126
215-635-6480
Hours: By appointment, Monday through Friday, 9 to 8 (Friday, in winter, 9 to 2); Sunday, 9 to 3.

This college, which bears the name of the beautiful Rebecca Gratz, does not, unhappily, have any exhibition or memorabilia to commemorate her.

However, there are 8 display cases, 38 historical pictures and documents, Signal Corps photographs of people at concentration camps, a Nazi humor magazine, and a letter to the United Nations, written on October 2, 1942, by a displaced person.

The collection of artifacts has some macabre items, such as a mace issued to the German home guard, a bull whip used at the camps, and a banjo made from a Torah scroll.

ETHNIC IMAGERY

THE BALCH INSTITUTE FOR ETHNIC
STUDIES/PHILADELPHIA JEWISH ARCHIVES CENTER
18 South Seventh Street
Philadelphia, PA 19106
215-925-8090
Hours: Balch, Monday through Saturday, 9 to 5; Archives, Monday through Friday, 9 to 5.

Some exhibits at the Balch Institute are bold and flashy, like the one I saw there in the 1980s: Ethnic Images in Advertising. It had stereotypes of everyone from black mammies and red-headed Irish boozers to Scots in tartans and Jews with crooked noses. These figures sold everything from pancakes to soap, but none of them topped the advertising campaign, during the 1960s, by Henry S. Levy & Sons to sell their Jewish rye bread. Blatant but not unpleasant ethnic images of every type except Jews were accompanied by the legend "You don't have to be Jewish to love Levy's." The interesting psychological effect, as the exhibit catalog said, was to communicate the message "You don't have to be Jewish to love Jews," and this result probably helped to clear the way for people to recognize the stupidity of prejudice and laugh at it.

More recent traveling exhibits assembled by the Balch Institute have presented Ethnic Images in the Comics and Something Old, Something New: Ethnic Weddings in America. The collection is multiethnic and, as the titles make clear, the themes are splendidly imaginative. The Institute's collection is made up of photographs, documents, letters, steamer trunks, ship manifests, clothing, posters, tablecloths, and family albums.

The Balches were a prominent Philadelphia family who designated their fortune to be used for a library. In 1957, trustees of their estate asked the Orphans' Court of Philadelphia, which oversees the execution of wills, for direction. Recognizing the importance of such a collection in our multiethnic nation, the court's recommendation was for a library devoted to the story of immigration and ethnicity in America.

Many Institute exhibits focus on quieter subjects than commercials and comics. Traditions in Transition: Jewish Culture in Philadelphia, 1840–1940 illustrated the life of Jews in the region through photographs, documents, and handbills. There was, for example, a document formally entitled "Application of Mother For Pension." The 60-year-old widow of Benjamin Hyneman, mother of Elias, lost her son, who was her sole support, on the 7th day of January, 1875. He died as a result of "cruel treatment and exposure" experienced while he was a prisoner of war at Andersonville, Georgia, during the Civil War. In quickly scratched penmanship, it was put forward that Rebekah Hyneman had depended on

"You don't have to be Jewish to love Levy's." © 1967 Henry S. Levy & Sons. Courtesy of the Balch Institute Collection.

friends and family for sustenance since her son's death. She signed her name to a statement that she "has not in any way been engaged in, or aided, or abetted the rebellion in the United States."

Another evocative document is incomprehensible to those who don't read Hebrew; only the title is in English: "The United Push Cart Peddler's Ass'n." The Philadelphia Jewish Archives Center was the donor.

A carefully hand-lettered page from a 1935 scrapbook of the Isabella Rosenbach Vacation School describes the D.O.R. (Daughters of Rebecca) Club, which numbered 37 children on its rolls. "What Our Name Means To Us" was the topic, and the text explained:

The name Rebecca brings to our mind two great ladies in Jewish history.

The first lady having been the wife of Isaac who was kind and as our Bible tells us, the Mother of thousands and ten thousands.

Then Rebecca Gratz who founded our fine Sunday School and who worked long and hard to instill into Jewish children a desire to learn more of our forefathers and to make us better Jews.

This is the beautiful Rebecca (see page 102) who was the model for the character in *Ivanhoe* and whose portrait was painted by Thomas Sully. The document used in the Balch exhibit belongs to the Rosenbach Library.

In the fall of 1992, to celebrate the 500th anniversary of Columbus's landing in America, the Balch Institute will host an exhibit that is scheduled to stay for five or six years: Discovering America; The Peopling of Pennsylvania. The exhibit will begin with immigrants' first contacts with Native Americans and will move forward to the present. Jewish immigration will be appropriately woven into the presentation.

Highlight: *The Philadelphia Jewish Archives Center at Balch Institute is a resource for the Institute's exhibits and for researchers interested in records of the Jewish community of Greater Philadelphia. For example, the Center holds historic records of Jewish organizations, social welfare agencies, and schools dating back to the early 19th century. There are many family papers and photographs.*

Portrait of Rebecca Gratz by Thomas Sully. Courtesy of The Rosenbach Museum & Library, Philadelphia, Pennsylvania.

◄ WASHINGTON SLEPT HERE ►

DESHLER-MORRIS HOUSE
5442 Germantown Avenue
Philadelphia, PA 19144
215-596-1748
Hours: April through December, Tuesday through Sunday, 1 to 4.

Isaac Franks was a New Yorker, the son of a wealthy Jewish merchant. He made a name for himself by volunteering for the Continental Army at the age of 17, and fighting heroically under General George Washington during the battle of Long Island. Wounded several times and captured, Franks was discharged in 1772.

Isaac Franks settled in Philadelphia and became wealthy. He opened a brokerage office and later was chief clerk of the Pennsylvania Supreme Court in 1819. He married a Christian woman and ceased to practice Judaism. The Franks house on High Street was nicely located between a house owned by George Washington and one owned by David Deshler. Franks was friendly with both of his Philadelphia neighbors.

David Deshler also owned a summer home in Germantown, a few miles outside Philadelphia. Originally a modest structure, he expanded it into a very fine residence in 1772. General William Howe made it his headquarters when his British forces occupied Philadelphia in 1777. When Deshler died in 1792, Isaac Franks bought Deshler's Germantown house to use as a summer residence.

The next year, a yellow fever epidemic raged through Philadelphia and took the lives of 4,000 people, one-tenth of the population of the city. To escape the epidemic, Franks moved his family to Bethlehem. He caught the fever, but was one of the fortunate few who survived it.

Because the Franks house in Germantown was empty, George and Martha Washington and their grandchildren, George Washington Parke Custis and his sister, Eleanor Parke Custis, rented it to escape the epidemic. There may have been a bit of a misunderstanding—Franks billed for $134.66 but was only paid $75.56—but the Washingtons rented the house again the next year, this time to escape the heat of the city in summer. Interestingly, the Franks moved out almost all of their furniture and the President brought his own, even though the First Family's stay in Germantown was a matter of just a month or so.

Isaac Franks died in 1822 and the house was sold out of his family. In July 1949, it became a cooperative venture of the National Park Service and Germantown Historical Society. It has been restored to resemble as closely as possible the way it might have looked during the period when Franks owned it and the Washingtons lived there. Part of the documentation for the furnishings was an inventory kept by Franks, although the only object that can be traced to him personally is a hand mirror. On the mantel in the parlor are four allegorical figures in porcelain representing the Four Continents; these may resemble "1 Sett Mantle China" recorded in Franks's inventory. When it is not on loan to another museum, a Gilbert Stuart portrait of Franks hangs above the mantel. The painting belongs to the Pennsylvania Academy of Fine Arts, but it is in great demand for exhibits that document American Judaism.

◆ IN AMERICA ◆

NATIONAL MUSEUM OF AMERICAN JEWISH HISTORY
Independence Mall East
55 North Fifth Street
Philadelphia, PA 19106
215-923-3811
Hours: Monday through Thursday, 10 to 5; Friday, 10 to 3;
Sunday, 12 to 5.

The Liberty Bell was important by design and became more so through circumstance. It was commissioned to hang in the statehouse for the colony of Pennsylvania. Modeled after "Great Tom" of Westminster, it was cast in Britain and arrived in Philadelphia on September 2, 1752. The bell weighed 2,080 pounds and was 12 feet in circumference. Part of the original inscription read: "Proclaim Liberty throughout all the Land unto the Inhabitants Thereof. Lev. XXV:10"—words spoken by the Lord to Moses, on Mount Sinai.

Although received in good order, the great brass bell broke the first time it was rung in the New World. Recast in Philadelphia and hoisted into the tower of the building we now call Independence Hall, it rang for the first public reading of the Declaration of Independence in July 1776. It was rung again in April 1783 to proclaim peace after the Revolutionary War, and, muffled, it tolled George Washington's death on December 18, 1799. In 1835, sounding for the funeral procession of Chief Justice John Marshall, it cracked again.

Today, the Liberty Bell is a national monument, a symbol of freedom for all to see if not hear. Its permanent location on Independence Square is just a few yards from the National Museum of American Jewish History—a fitting proximity because the Liberty Bell was carried to America in a ship owned by a Jewish merchant.

From coast to coast and north to south in this country, we find Jewish collections, if not museums, that have local predispositions. At a certain moment, someone seems to have stopped to wonder how we all got here, and then set about backtracking. That is true to some extent in the National Museum of American Jewish History, for a lot of Philadelphia is present at this museum. But, more important, this museum insistently narrates the story of Jewish participation in the growth and development of the Americas. The threads that stitch together regional collections and connections are pulled together here through a permanent exhibit called The American Jewish Experience, a chronological survey with three components: a time line, artifacts, and a video program.

The time line puts events into context. To understand why Jews first came to this part of the world, one must know that, when they were expelled from Spain by Queen Isabella and King Ferdinand in 1492 (at the same time Columbus was sent across the seas), many of the 150,000 Spanish Jews, forced to convert to Christianity, eventually made their way to Portugal and to Portuguese colonies such as those in Brazil.

When the relatively tolerant Dutch conquered the colony in Recife, Brazil, in 1630, it became possible for these Jews to resume their ancestral religion. Many did, and their settlements expanded. This period, at the beginning of the time line, is illustrated with the earliest available documentation of a New World Jewish community—the record book of the congregations Sur (Rock of) Israel and Magen (Shield of) Abraham of Recife and neighboring Mauricia. The book is written in Portuguese, with flourishing capital letters and elegant calligraphic script. One hundred and seventy one people signed this record.

Among the signers were 23 people who left for New Amsterdam in 1654—the Portuguese had reconquered the Recife colony and the Jews had to seek safety abroad. In New Amsterdam, they formed the first Jewish community in North America. The records of that congregation are today at Yeshiva University's museum in New York City (see page 79).

Along the line we find Jacob I. Cohen and Isaac Isaacs, who reappear later in Richmond, Virginia (page 182). The partners hired the legendary frontiersman Daniel Boone to survey land in Kentucky for them. Boone signed a receipt for the work and a note from him reports: "No doubt you are desirous your land business should be dunn but that is a thing inposible without money, and yours and Mr. Isaacs' will amount to a smart sum." (These communications from Boone are reproductions; originals are at the Library of Congress.)

Most Jews supported the American Revolution. Isaac Franks (see page 103) was an illustrious patriot. Gilbert Stuart's portrait of Franks shows him with the ruddy cheeks, highlighted by a white cravat, that were the artist's signature. An oil painting of the Franks house in Germantown which President George Washington rented is on display.

A copy of a letter Thomas Jefferson sent to Mordecai Manuel Noah, the original of which is at Yeshiva (see page 79) is in the collection. Noah, at one time Consul to Tunis, was a journalist, a sheriff, a playwright and publisher, and the first native-born American Jew to achieve national prominence. His scheme to create a homeland for Jews in New York State (see page 53) failed, but the indomitable Noah turned his attention to Palestine as a national home for Jews. Two of his public addresses on the subject, delivered in 1844, are on display.

Featured are works by the painter-photographer-adventurer-writer Solomon Nuñes Carvalho, who is commemorated by The Jewish Historical Society of Maryland (see page 21). This museum has a reproduction of his Incidents of Travel and Adventure in the Far West, With Col. Fremont's Last Expedition Across the Rocky Mountains: Including Three Months' Residence in Utah and a Perilous Trip Across the Great American to the Pacific, as well as some of his portraits of Jews and Indians.

Michel Goldwasser, later Goldwater, was a Polish émigré who set sail for America in 1851. "Big Mike" Goldwasser and his brother "Little Joe" pioneered and made their fortune in Arizona. Mike's wife stayed in more civilized San Francisco, where he visited her during religious holidays. When Mike retired in 1855, he rejoined his wife, with whom he then lived for 18 years. Their son, Baron, married out of the Jewish faith, and his son Barry was an Episcopalian. Barry Goldwater was the Republican candidate for President of the United States in 1964, the first and only presidential candidate with known Jewish ancestry.

The time line marches on, weaving artifacts with events and personalities with history, making connection after connection, moving toward the discovery of a formula, an equation, a pattern that might make the past eras orderly rather than chaotic, harmonious rather than cacaphonic, or—at least—comprehensible.

Besides its permanent exhibit, the National Museum of American Jewish History hosts and organizes temporary exhibitions. Topics are varied, as this selection of titles reveals: Pioneers and Adventurers—Jews Across the Plains and Rockies; Legacy of Laughter—Jewish Humor; Pictures for the Book of Life—Jewish New Year Cards, 1870–1940; Hanukkah Lamp Showcase. There are frequent exhibits of contemporary art and artifacts.

Highlight: *In a photograph dated 1869, gazing straight into the camera with seriousness befitting their high stations are chiefs Sitting Bull, Swift Bear, Spotted Tail, and Red Cloud—and Julius Meyer, who was adopted by the Ponca Indians. They called him Curly-head White Chief One Tongue. Born in Germany, Meyer became an Indian interpreter, a dealer, and an entrepreneur. He accompanied a troupe of Indians on one of Buffalo Bill's tours of Europe.*

❧ THE LURE OF LITERATURE ❧

THE ROSENBACH MUSEUM & LIBRARY
2010 DeLancey Place
Philadelphia, PA 19103
215-732-1600
Hours: Tuesday through Sunday, 11 to 4; closed in August.

During his lifetime, Dr. Abraham Simon Wolf Rosenbach was the most successful rare book dealer the world had ever known. His brother, Philip, was an art collector and dealer. Between them, they assembled an extraordinary collection of books, manuscripts, works of art on paper, and decorative arts. Their personal collections are now, in large part, at The Rosenbach Museum & Library, a discreet, four-story townhouse built in 1866.

The two brothers lived there, and it is furnished with items from the art and antiques business of the Rosenbach Company. Some of the exhibit cases scattered throughout the building may seem quite eccentric. For instance, poet Marianne Moore's living room is just across the hall from Dr. Rosenbach's library. The Rosenbachs had bought her archives in 1968. In her will, she left the contents of the room to the museum, stipulating that it be arranged exactly as it was when she had lived in it in Greenwich Village.

Dr. Rosenbach, president of the American Friends of the Hebrew University, the American Jewish Historical Society, and Gratz College, a bibliophile and scholar, was not universally loved, as this verse by James Joyce makes all too clear:

> *Rosy Brook he bought a book*
> *Though he didn't know how to spell it.*
> *Such is the lure of literature*
> *To the lad who can buy and sell it.*

Joyce was complaining because his longhand manuscript of *Ulysses*, auctioned off in January 1924, had been bought by Rosenbach. Joyce was annoyed mostly because Rosenbach had paid a mere $1,975; Joseph Conrad's manuscript for *Victory* went for four times that amount. The manuscript for *Ulysses* is in this museum.

The collection once had substantially more Judaica than it does now; Dr. Rosenbach donated generously to the Jewish Theological Seminary and the American Jewish Historical Society. These are some of the important items that remain:

- A Hebrew Bible dated July 8 to August 6, 1491. This is the second Portuguese Pentateuch (and the first printed in Lisbon) printed on vellum. As its colophon says, "As for its elegance and preciousness, white marble, alabaster and pearls cannot be compared therewith, nor the gold of Parvim." The box made to hold this bible is of red Cordova leather tooled with interlacing geometrical designs and heavy brass details.

- An even earlier bible, indeed the earliest printing of the Pentateuch in Hebrew of which complete copies are known. This one is dated January 25, 1482.

- The book that gave the Hebrew alphabet its debut in the Western Hemisphere: *The Whole Booke of Psalmes; Faithfully Translated into English Metre. Whereunto is pre-fixed a discourse declaring not only the lawfullness, but also the necessity of the heavenly Ordinance of singing Scripture Psalmes in the Churches of God.* Dated 1640, this is the earliest extant book printed in America, an original metrical translation of the Book of Psalms, in which Psalm 119 is in Hebrew. Only 1,700 copies of the book were printed; 11 have survived and this is one of 3 still in their original bindings.

- Gratz family portraits, including a Thomas Sully portrait of Rebecca done the year after the portrait owned by the Delaware Art Museum (see page 3). Although over fifty, Rebecca looks younger and more beautiful than ever.

- Another Sully portrait, of Benjamin Gratz, Rebecca's brother, and portraits of Miriam and Michael Gratz, Rebecca's and Benjamin's parents, done by Sully's daughter, Jane Cooper Sully Darley. There is also a portrait by John Wesley Jarvis of Aaron Levy, a Revolutionary patriot and the founder of Aaronsburg, Pennsylvania. Levy was the great-great-uncle of the Rosenbach brothers and he named Simon Gratz, another of Rebecca's brothers, as his heir.

Highlight: *The Rosenbach Museum has a cadre of trained docents who guide visitors through the collection. Group tours are made by special arrangement. It would be useful to call in advance to make your interests known; a tour tailored more specifically to your curiosity might then be arranged.*

～ FRANKLIN AND FRIENDS ～

THE LIBRARY COMPANY OF PHILADELPHIA
1314 Locust Street
Philadelphia, PA 19107
215-546-3181
Hours: Monday through Friday, 9 to 4:45.

The illustrious Dr. A. S. W. Rosenbach, collector extraordinary, published a book of his own in 1926: *An American Jewish Bibliography; Being a list of books and pamphlets by or relating to them printed in the United States from the establishment of the press in the colonies until 1850.* For a title that promising, the bibliography is relatively meager—only about 700 books. Not many books had been published in the United States by then, and little of what did get printed was concerned with Jews. Those 700 books are now very rare and most of them are at the Library Company of Philadelphia.

The Company itself is pretty rare. It was founded by Benjamin Franklin and a group of his friends in 1731. They bought books with the annual contributions made by each shareholder. Requests for specific titles were written on a piece of paper that was folded up and slipped inside the "Lion's Mouth," the lion having been painted on the front of a box.

This was the largest public library in North America through the middle of the 19th century. It is the only major colonial American library that has survived with its collection virtually intact. Its quarters have changed several times. First, the library was in someone's house; for a time, it was in Independence Hall. Today, it is in a new, fireproof building in the center of Philadelphia, one block east of the Academy of Music. An independent research library, its collections document every aspect of the history and background of American culture from the colonial period to the Civil War. The rare book collection is of national importance: its holdings number 450,000 books, 50,000 graphics, and 160,000 manuscripts.

Among the rarest volumes in The Library Company collection are the first Hebrew grammar printed in America (dated 1735), and what is believed to be the first Jewish prayer book, published in 1760.

There is also a volume written by a Jewish doctor and pharmacist, David de Isaac Cohen Nassy, published during the yellow fever epidemic of 1793: *Treatise on Yellow Fever; Observations on the Cause, Nature & Treatment of the Epidemic Disorder Prevalent in Philadelphia*. Not only was it the first medical book written by a Jew in America, but Nassy's treatments were, apparently, more successful than those of his more famous contemporary, Dr. Benjamin Rush, with whom he disagreed.

In the collection of drawings is one by George Catlin of Mordecai Manuel Noah, already encountered several times in this book. Catlin did portraits for a time early in his career, but he became famous for devoting his artistic talent and passion to recording the life and ways of the American Indian.

The manuscript collection also holds a bill for 1238 pounds 5 shillings 7½ pence (colonial currency) for blankets, handkerchiefs, tomahawks, looking glasses, and wampum sold by an Indian trader to Simon, Levy and Company at Fort Pitt on March 23rd, 1765.

The extensive collection of American Judaica at The Library Company of Philadelphia is among the most significant in the country. Although it is a library rather than a museum, there is always an exhibit relating to some phase of the collection.

Highlight: *In a letter written by Naphtali Phillips to John A. McAllister on October 24, 1868, is a description of Philadelphia's Grand Federal Procession of 1788, a celebration of the state's ratification of the Constitution. Phillips had witnessed that procession and recalled it vividly eighty years later. At the end of the parade, he noted, "There was a number of long tables loaded with all kinds of provisions with a separate table for the Jews who could not partake of the meats from the other tables but they had a full supply of soused salmon, bread and crackers, almonds, raisins, etc."*

❂ DECORATIVE ARTS ❁

PHILADELPHIA MUSEUM OF ART
26th Street & Benjamin Franklin Parkway
Philadelphia, PA
Mailing address: P.O. Box 7646
Philadelphia, PA 19101-7646
215-763-8100
Hours: Tuesday through Sunday, 10 to 5.

The Gratz family of Philadelphia was one of the city's most prominent families. Bernard and Michael Gratz settled in Pennsylvania in the 1750s. They were merchants whose business dealings stretched from the Caribbean to the American frontier towns, which they helped to develop. They kept the Continental Army in supplies, clothing, and ammunition, and often didn't receive payment. Observant Jews who were active in their congregations and in building Philadelphia's first synagogue, Mikeveh Israel, they were also patriotic Americans.

In the American Decorative Arts Gallery of this museum, among the late Federal and early Empire furnishings, you will find a sideboard and matching knife boxes, a secretary-bookcase, and a celarette (wine case) that belonged to a descendant of the Gratzes, Simon Gratz. The furnishings were made for him by a Philadelphia cabinetmaker, Joseph Barry, of mahogany veneer inlaid with brass and ebony, a style that was popular in England in the early years of the 19th century.

Highlight: *Guides at the Philadelphia Museum of Art schedule tours that look specifically at the works of Jewish artists in the collection. Such tours are planned several weeks in advance. To inquire whether such a tour is available or may be arranged, call the Group Sales Office, 215-787-5498.*

RHODE ISLAND

❦ SINCE 1759 ❧

TOURO SYNAGOGUE, NATIONAL HISTORIC SITE
85 Touro Street
Newport, RI 02840
401-847-4794
Hours: Closed on Saturday. Sunday through Friday: May through mid-June, 1 to 3; mid-June to Labor Day, 10 to 5; Labor Day through September, 1 to 3. October through May, Sunday only, 1 to 3.

Touro Synagogue is the oldest synagogue building in the United States. Ground was broken for it on August 1, 1759, and the building was dedicated on December 2, 1763.

From the street, one sees a square, limewashed brick building with deep-set, arched windows. The wood trim is painted a soft, rosy brown. The impression given by the exterior is one of simple, quiet dignity. Inside, that feeling is overwhelming.

I stood on the second-story balcony, the women's balcony, and looked around. The walls are white and the woodwork is a soft grey. The balcony is supported by twelve columns, representing the twelve tribes of Israel. Each column is believed to be a full tree. These columns have the plain scroll of Ionic capitals for ornament. In discreet but lovely contrast, the columns that reach from the balcony to the ceiling, tapering slightly toward the top, have feathery, Corinthian capitals. Such details bespeak the skill of the architect, Peter Harrison, who was well-known in his day. He had never designed a synagogue before. Harrison was also a navigator and merchant.

According to Bernard Kusinitz, president of the Congregation Jeshuat Israel (Salvation of Israel), which worships in Touro Synagogue to this day, the building is a "masterpiece of creative adaptation." Harrison was able to put together this masterpiece by combining the requirements of his clients with the designs he researched through his own important architectural library. "He used all kinds of ideas, none original, but he put them all together in an original way," Kusinitz said.

There is no record of Harrison's ever having been paid for his design of Touro; common belief is that he did it as a labor of love. It transmits a sense of personal devotion. Built of brick imported from England, the building is angled to allow the holy ark to be oriented east, toward Jerusalem.

Harrison, who was not a Jew, had no specific model on which to base his details, but the floor plan is that of a typical Sephardic synagogue, probably as remembered and described to the architect by Isaac Touro, who had come to Newport from Amsterdam. Fixtures, such as four of the five chandeliers, and architectural details, such as the fanlight windows, are colonial.

The noncolonial central chandelier is an 18th-century rococo extravaganza with twelve branches, decorated with what look like tiny monks' heads. One legend is that it was made by a Marrano monk (a Spanish Jew forced to convert to Catholicism). Kusinitz has asked specialists at the Art Institute of Chicago and the Metropolitan Museum of Art to look at this chandelier, but all they can tell him is that they've never seen another like it. How it got to this country is a mystery.

In a wooden case on the balustrade, above the entrance, is a round wall clock that has brass works. Made in England in 1769, it is still running. And still burning, in a manner of speaking, is the Ner Tamid, the eternal light in front of the ark. When the synagogue was new, the light was fueled with oil. When electricity was installed around the turn of the century, a small electric bulb was substituted for the wick.

One prized possession of the Congregation rests in a glass case beside the ark: a Torah, written on deerskin and now about 500 years old. Inside the ark are more Torahs, two of which are crowned with beautiful and important silverwork: two sets of rimmonim, finials with bells, by the famous silversmith Myer Meyers.

Born in 1723, Meyers was the first Jewish artisan to take advantage of an act passed in 1716 by the colonial legislature of New York permitting Jews to practice the profession of their choice. In his lifetime, Meyers made six sets of Torah bells.

Although Touro Synagogue was built in 1759, the Jewish congregation that settled Newport had arrived 100 years earlier. They were mainly Marranos—Spanish and Portuguese Jews who pretended to convert to Christianity to avoid persecution, and who had been living in the West Indies, where trade with Newport was active. They believed they would be able to settle without fear in the colony of Rhode Island and the Providence Plantations because its founder, Roger Williams, had publicly declared himself a champion of freedom of religion.

Touro Synagogue was closed to worshippers during the Revolutionary War; Newport was occupied by the British on December 8, 1776. It became the meeting place of the Rhode Island General Assembly from 1781 to 1784. George Washington visited Newport a few times. He is known to have come in 1781, when a town meeting was held in the building.

Moses Seixas (1744–1809) was a prominent Newport businessman and Warden of Congregation Jeshuat Israel. When the British sacked the city, Seixas decided not to leave, although many other patriots did. Later, he wrote to President Washington on behalf of the Congregation, stressing the importance of a government dedicated to freedom of worship.

In return, Seixas received a letter from Washington that embodied the new nation's principles of religious freedom but, in fact, adapted Seixas's own words. Washington wrote, in part: ". . . happily the Government of the United States which gives to bigotry no sanction, to persecution no assistance requires only that they who live under its protection should demean themselves as good citizens in giving it on all occasions their effectual support." A facsimile of the letter is posted on a wall of the synagogue. (The original is at the B'nai B'rith museum in Washington; see page 5.)

After being closed for a number of years, Touro synagogue was reopened on August 2, 1850. It was restored with funds from a bequest of Abraham Touro, Isaac's son. It has operated as a place of worship ever since and has become one of the important landmarks for Jews of the world.

Highlight: *Although the Touro Synagogue itself is a museum, some items of interest are displayed across the street in the Jewish Community Center. The small collection includes a portrait of Abraham Touro, who died in 1822, possibly painted by Gilbert Stuart. Touro's* *handwritten will as well as letters from Harry Truman and Dwight D. Eisenhower are in the museum.*

There is also a perplexing contraption that looks like a table but stands only about a foot off the ground. Its surface measures some three and one-half by four feet, and it has a stick or pole attached. It is a matzo board, also known as an Omer board, and was made of Palestinian olive wood at the beginning of the 20th century. It was used in the preparation of dough for matzos used in the Passover season.

❧ WHERE TO START? ❧

TEMPLE EMANU-EL
99 Taft Avenue
Providence, RI 02906
401-331-1616
Hours: By appointment.

I have visited hundreds of museums and, although none is quite like any other, most share a chronic complaint: not enough space. Nowhere is the problem more evident than in this museum. It is bursting its seams with an eclectic collection of treasures, but its crowdedness is part of its charm. The room housing the museum when I visited could not have been much larger than 10 by 15 feet, but it was rich with fascinating objects.

The effect was like that of a typical Victorian cabinet of curiosities: stunning, but where to start? Holidays and other themes give an organizational rhyme and reason. These are some of the things that caught my attention:

- An Oriental wall hanging, roughly five feet by three feet, woven in 1915, in browns, beiges, and light blue. Menorahs are the motif and the word Zion is woven in Hebrew.
- Rebecca Rosenthal's wedding dress, of beige and cream-colored silk, with three large bows on the bodice and a lot of ruffles. Rebecca was the first Jewish woman to graduate from Hunter College. When she married in 1875, she wore this dress with the high-button matching shoes that are on the

floor next to it. Around her neck was a locket containing pictures of her parents.

- A variety of menorahs from Holland, Poland, Austria, and Italy. Their shiny brass or silver is set off by a collection of tiny clay lamps from Israel. These oil lamps, from recently excavated sites, date back to the 3rd to 7th century B.C.E.

- A mizrach, a visually attractive ornament that is placed on an east wall to show the direction of Jerusalem. This marvelous mizrach is a plate more than 15 inches in diameter. It is painted, in bright colors, with a perplexing mis-en-scène: A warrior in his suit of mail stands with his lance in the fore-ground. A lion rests quite placidly near his feet. An idyllic, rolling landscape with palm trees recedes to the horizon, dotted along the way with a castle here and there. On the horizon, rising in a blaze of light, is a Star of David.

- A piece of rock with a plant imprint so delicate it is nearly incredible. The card says that this was "pictured in the Foot-steps of Moses"—information that only serves to heighten the mystery.

- A 2 by 3¾-inch hand-lettered and illustrated daily prayer book, its pages worn from turning. It is an Omer book, used to count the days from the end of Passover to Shabuoth.

Highlight: *Among the finest in the country, the collection is in a handsome, imposing building that was constructed in 1927 for Provi-dence's first Conservative congregation. Pieces from the collection, including works of art on paper, are on view throughout the Temple. Emanu-El, which is also frequently spelled Emanuel, means "God is with us."*

❧ LOOK CAREFULLY ❧

THE RHODE ISLAND JEWISH HISTORICAL ASSOCIATION
130 Sessions Street
Providence, RI 02906
401-331-1360
Hours: Monday, Tuesday, and Thursday, 10 to 1:30, and by
appointment.

This is an archetypical small historic society. If you walk in un-
prepared, you might quickly walk out again. It's a very small room—
an office, really—with desks, file cabinets, old trophies, signs from
buildings long gone, wrinkled pictures, plaques, and certificates on
the walls.

If you are lucky enough, you will run into someone like Association president Robert Kotlen. He'll tell you, for example, to look
carefully at the long photograph taken, in 1916, on the steps of the
state house. It's a lineup of members of the Providence Workmen's
Beneficial Association. Describing how a photographer at that time
used to take such a panorama, Kotlen points out that the little boy on
the far left of the scene is also standing at the far right. He ran in back
and emerged at the far end by the time the camera had it in focus.

An old menorah is distinguished not by intrinsic beauty, but by
the fact that the man who owned it used to work for John F. Fitzgerald ("Honey Fitz"), John F. Kennedy's maternal grandfather, when
Fitzgerald was mayor of Boston. The man used to take his candle
holder to Town Hall for the Friday evening lighting ceremony.

Highlight: *Don't miss the faded mannequin that one of Kotlen's
relatives used to parade, in the back of a wagon, to Boston and all
around town, dressed in the high fashion of the era (1890 to 1910) to
advertise the wares of his clothing company. A strange white cone on
top of a filing cabinet is a 22.2-pound "lump" of sugar, one of two
brought to Providence by a Russian woman who wasn't sure she'd be
able to find sugar in the New World. Although they are separate
entities, the Association is in a building across the street from the
Jewish Community Center of Rhode Island, a part of which has been
sectioned off for a Holocaust Museum. There are changing exhibits at
the JCC, sometimes built on material collected from local members
and sometimes rented as traveling exhibits.*

❤ MATERIAL CULTURE ∝

TEMPLE BETH-EL
70 Orchard Avenue
Providence, RI 02906
401-331-6070
Hours: Monday through Thursday, 9 to 5; Friday, 9 to 3. Advance
arrangements are recommended.

On June 13, 1955, *LIFE* magazine focused on Judaism in its
series of articles on the World's Greatest Religions. Temple Beth-El
of Providence was chosen to represent the Jewish Reform movement. It was then in a brand new building, dedicated just a year
earlier. The modern (and at that time controversial) design was by
Percival Goodman, an architect who would go on to build his reputation on synagogue design. Though one of his earliest, this is also
one of his best works.

In contrast to the collection of ritual and ceremonial objects at
nearby Emanu-El, Beth-El displays, in attractive wall cases, the mun-
dane objects of daily life that we often use and throw away.

A World War II relic, a USO Kit of Religious Materials for a
Jewish Service Man, includes a Jewish Calendar for Soldiers and
Sailors for the year 1944 and a tiny mezuzah. In the collection are
more than 300 letters and cards from service men and women. The
Temple's president had been a World War II pilot.

Collecting souvenirs is an ancient human trait; mistrusting our
memories, we are forever seeking ways to hold on to images we have
seen, especially from places we are leaving. A little box of seeds and a
book of pressed flowers from the Holy Land were among the 350
items on display when I visited. There were Hanukkah cards and
many other touching souvenirs.

The exhibits' fascination has resulted from the exhibition skills
of archivist George Goodwin. His idea is to illustrate the lives of the
people in the congregation through everyday objects which, as he
presents them, take on the weight and value of what art historians
call material culture—the rich, narrative, historic value of contemporary possessions.

Highlight: *I was impressed with Harold Sidney's Boy Scout uniform
and counted 27 patches on the sleeve of the scout shirt he wore in 1923.*

COLORADO

❧ WHITE PLAGUE ❧

ISAAC SOLOMON SYNAGOGUE AND MUSEUM
AMC Cancer Research Center
1600 Pierce Street
Denver, CO 80214
303-233-6501
Hours: Tour of the grounds and museum, by appointment.

In 1904, the Jewish Consumptives' Relief Society (JCRS) was established to care for victims of tuberculosis. Patients came from all parts of the United States. In those days, TB was known as the "white plague" and it was ravaging America's cities.

The JCRS began with eight patients, seven tents, and a one-story frame building as its headquarters. It grew into a self-sufficient community that had its own dairy, poultry farm, general store, post office, library, and other facilities. The fresh, dry Colorado air was the treatment of choice and patients were kept isolated in small sheds or tents.

By 1954, the development of successful drug treatment for tuberculosis caused the mission of the institution to change, and it is now a leading cancer research facility. Many of the original buildings have been preserved (the center is on the National Register of Historic Places) and a tour of the campus gives a fascinating glimpse of the past.

The first synagogue was built on the campus in 1911, but it was destroyed by fire and rebuilt in 1925. In 1981, the Isaac Solomon Synagogue and Museum was opened, and artifacts from the early history of the institution were put on display.

Highlight: *The synagogue is a low, red brick building made somewhat eccentric by a neo-Gothic window design. Although it could seat 70 worshippers, it is no longer used for religious services. Among the items on display is a well-preserved Torah from the JCRS days.*

❧ GOLDA ❧

GOLDA MEIR HOUSE
1020 Ninth Street Historic Park
Auraria Higher Education Center Campus
Auraria Foundation
Mailing address: Campus Box A
P.O. Box 173361
Denver, CO 80217-3361
303-556-2259

In 1913 when G. was fifteen she wrote me in one of her letters that she wants to leave home and without her parents' permission to come to Denver and finish high school, and prepare herself to enter teachers' college. . . . The parents' room was on the second floor over the store of the shop with a side window to the roof. Her girlfriend, Regina Hamburger, waited under the window. This was in the evening. G. tied a cord to the suitcase and let it down through the window where the girlfriend took it over. They both took it to the train station and left it in the baggage department. The next day G. woke up in the morning, left a note in which she took leave of her parents and asked them to forgive her for the grief, sorrow etc. that she brought on them.

In these circumstances, Goldie Mabowitz left home in Milwaukee, in 1913, and went to live with her sister, in Denver. Her sister's memoirs record the event. Goldie's parents wanted her to stay home and get married, but she wanted to be a teacher. She became the Prime Minister of Israel. She changed her name to Golda Meir along the way.

Golda lived with her sister, Sheyna, who had moved to Denver for the TB cure, in a brick duplex. She went to North High School for almost three years.

In 1989, a group of volunteers from North High School painted Golda's former home after it had been saved from destruction (for the second time) and moved onto the Auraria campus where it now proudly stands. Getting it there had been a struggle marked by legal battles, vandalism, fires, swastikas, and political controversy. Finally, the efforts of the Auraria Foundation, established in 1983 to support education and historic projects, raised enough money to move the building onto the campus.

While the house, adorned with a huge red, white, and blue ribbon, was being moved on a flatbed in 1988, there were festivities—Israeli folk dancing and speeches. The mayor proclaimed September 25 Golda Meir House Day and Rep. Pat Schroeder, a Colorado Democrat, said, looking at the flatbed, "This is where she set her course. She showed that you could do something in this community that translated globally."

"This home is where she decided what she was going to do with her life," Larry Ambrose of the Auraria Foundation told the students painting the trim of the red brick duplex. Many of the public-spirited students didn't know who Golda Meir was, before they got involved in the restoration. But, as one student cheerily told a reporter between brush strokes, "Now I'm informed."

Members of the Auraria Foundation are still trying to raise money (about $70,000 is needed) to carry out their plans of opening the house as a museum, documenting how Golda Meir came to Denver, and displaying the memorabilia from her life that they have been collecting.

Highlight: *When the house was brought onto the campus, it was a scabrous mess. The white paint that had covered the red brick was peeling, windows and doors were boarded up, and the vermin could almost be heard scratching around inside. Today, the brick has been restored; the discreetly detailed trim, white railings, and columns supporting the entry porch are freshly painted; and the house speaks of an earnest, working-class past and a commendable contemporary devotion.*

❧ ROCKY MOUNTAIN CHAI ❧

MIZEL MUSEUM OF JUDAICA
560 South Monaco Parkway
Denver, CO 80224
303-333-4156
Hours: Monday through Thursday, 10 to 4; Sunday, 10 to noon.

Landlocked, rectangular, and our most mountainous state (average elevation 6,790 feet), Colorado has also been, since World War II, one of the fastest growing. Eighty percent of its 3.3 million population is urban, and 1.7 million live in metropolitan Denver; of these, 45,000 are Jews. The influx started with the Colorado gold rush 130 years ago. Among the adventurers were about a dozen Jews, primarily German immigrants. Some may have panned for gold, but others did the essential work of keeping the prospectors supplied with the necessities of life, from clothing to cash.

Jewish history in the region includes the rescue of a group of immigrants who had been tricked into settling the barren mountains near the Arkansas River. Otto Mears, known as "the Hebrew pathfinder" and a "president maker," built a network of roads and then went to Washington. According to folklore, he spoke Ute, the Native American language, with a Yiddish accent.

An important Jewish museum is appropriate in Denver. The Mizel Museum of Judaica was established in 1982. Besides lending their name to the museum, the Mizels contributed funds that enabled the purchase of an extremely interesting collection of 40 works produced in Palestine between approximately 1910 and 1930. A few examples are: a Mahzor or prayer book with elaborately embossed leather binding, a miniature painting on enamel of Abraham as a shepherd, Hanukkah lamps, and a Megillah scroll in an elegant filigree silver case.

A major acquisition for the museum has been Judaica from the Bezalel School, an academy of arts and crafts founded in Jerusalem, in 1906, by Boris Schatz (1867–1932). Explorers of Jewish art soon discover Schatz, an artist favored at the Bulgarian court. His dream was to start an art center in the Holy Land. His association with Theodore Herzl, the founder of political Zionism and the World Zionist Organization, and the support Herzl was able to mobilize at the Seventh Zionist Congress of 1905, plus financial backing from banker/philanthropist Otto Warburg, enabled Schatz to see his dream come true. Palestine was, at the turn of the century, a backward, desolate place with little cultural life and few Jews in residence. Shatz's vision and persistence brought the institution to realization.

Why the Bezalel School? The name is from Exodus: "And the Lord spoke unto Moses, saying: 'See, I have called by name Bezalel . . . and I have filled him with the spirit of God, in wisdom and in understanding, and in knowledge, and in all manner of workmanship, to devise skilful works, to work in gold, and in silver, and in brass, and in cutting of stones for setting, and in carving of wood, to work in all manner of workmanship.'" The connection was plain and direct. To round it out, Boris Schatz named his son Bezalel, and his son became an artist. The Bezalel School has had an erratic history over the cataclysmic events of this century, but it still exists.

The Mizel Museum's collection of Judaica from Bezalel, after its assembly and exhibition in Denver, went traveling to other galleries, and the Mizel continues to put together a series of intriguing exhibits. For example, one exhibit was devoted to maps of the Holy Land produced during the Golden Age of Cartography (1498 to 1800). To a large extent, those early map makers used their imagination to embellish whatever landfalls they had attained at sea and from high elevations. Ancient maps, in some of which a country may have been represented in the shape of an animal or in architectural forms, are creations of imagination and art.

Other works of art exhibited at the museum are portraits and landscapes, from Europe to Palestine, by Hermann Struck, a graphic artist, master etcher, and lithographer. He too settled in Israel and was a great teacher whose name is now synonymous with development of the artistic and cultural life of that country. Struck died in 1944.

Highlight: *Currently housed in a synagogue, the Mizel is the only museum of Judaica in the Rocky Mountain region, and the staff devotes considerable energy to showing visitors the local flavor of Jewish history. The Hebrew word chai means life. It is a symbol that is often worn as a talisman on a pendant.*

❧ WESTERN CIVILIZATION ❧

IRA M. BECK MEMORIAL ARCHIVES OF ROCKY
MOUNTAIN JEWISH HISTORY
University of Denver
Denver, CO 80208-0292
303-871-3020
Hours: Monday through Friday by appointment (generally, 8:30 to
2:30).

S. Cohen's General Store in Fairplay, Colorado, was photographed in 1885 as the background; two couples, four children of assorted sizes, and a woman were lined up on the sidewalk in front. The women are in long dresses and the men wear hats (one sports a bowler). The bricks of the building are so well defined by the mortar around them that they can be counted, except where a wide swath has been painted across the front and lettered with the advice "Clothing & Boots, GROCERIES and Miners Supplies Always on Hand."

In another photo, Max Stein's horse is in the background. Max, a handsome man with a bushy dark mustache, is dressed in his uniform, which has a big bright star on the left side. He was a mounted policeman in Pueblo, Colorado, at the turn of the century.

Colorful, appealing, and instructive, the history of the Jewish experience in the states of Idaho, Montana, Wyoming, Colorado, and New Mexico is the focus of this historical and archival collection, an affiliate of the Center for Judaic Studies at the University of Denver. The programs sponsored are varied and include exhibits, meetings, and research projects, as well as field trips to places of regional Jewish historical interest. In the collection of over a million documents are manuscripts, periodicals, oral histories, newspapers, artifacts, memorabilia, and over 3,000 photos.

Highlight: *The Rocky Mountain region is rich in Jewish history and, although there is no specific exhibition space at the university, small exhibits are put together for other organizations. The archives, housed at Penrose Library and the Center for Judaic Studies, are available for research by appointment.*

FLORIDA

◆ SUNSHINE STATE ◆

MOSAIC, JEWISH LIFE IN FLORIDA
c/o Marcia Kerstein Zerivitz
635 Mariner Way
Altamonte Springs, FL 32701-5420
407-834-8576
Hours: Call for new location and information.

In a photograph, little Felix Glickstein is astride a yawning (or yelping) alligator. Felix is the epitome of toddler fashion à la 1916, in his white leggings, black shoes, and hat with a pom pom. If pictures can be worth a thousand words, this is one of those pictures.

To understand the significance of a particular 19th-century Torah, however, words are essential. One must read how Marcus Joseph Weinkle was called up for the Russian army in 1887. Weinkle died of a fever soon afterward, his family announced. They buried him, very carefully. In the dark of night he rose from his grave, dressed in the clothes hidden nearby, and fled. He made his way to Jaffa, Palestine, via Turkey. In 1890, Weinkle arrived in America. He settled in Florida, where he married, opened a lumber mill, had two children, and used the family Torah from Russia.

Weinkle's Torah, a photo taken of him in Jaffa to show his family he had arrived safely, and the picture of Felix Glickstein (the alligator was stuffed, by the way) are among the evocative memorabilia that are part of the MOSAIC exhibition. First shown in January 1991, it is traveling throughout Florida until the end of 1992. Thereafter, it may go to Washington, DC, to Israel, and elsewhere. The expectation is that, eventually, it will be permanently installed in a museum. The exhibition began as a Fort Lauderdale senior center project sponsored by the local Jewish Community Center.

The history of Jews in Florida, to the surprise of most people who believe it spans barely 50 years, began in 1763 in Pensacola, where the state's first synagogue was built. It is thought that Jews

Felix Glickstein astride an alligator. Courtesy of MOSAIC.

came with Ponce de Leon in the 1500s, but without documentation that arrival remains speculative. Florida's first U.S. senator, who took office in 1845, was Jewish, as was the founder of the Florida Cattlemen's Association.

Marcia Kerstein Zerivitz, state coordinator and development director for the exhibition, spent three years and traveled 100,000 miles to gather information; she met hundreds of individuals and found relatives of people who didn't know they had them. She also collected 5,000 photographs. The exhibition is a great success and fascinates non-Floridians as well as natives. Stories about the lives of Jews, so often stories of courage and persistence and victory, are not without romance.

Helene Herskowitz was born and grew up in Miami. When her mother died in 1985, she inherited a collection of love letters that her grandfather in Key West had written to his sweetheart in Atlanta during the late 1890s. The sweetheart became his wife, and those letters provided Ms. Herskowitz a great insight not only into the personalities of her grandparents but also into the events and texture of the times and places in which they lived. The family is one of those documented by MOSAIC.

Highlight: *Don't overlook the 19th-century jewelry salesman's sample kit that belonged to Michael Schops.*

ᕤ MEMORIAL ᕤ

HOLOCAUST MEMORIAL RESOURCE AND EDUCATION CENTER OF CENTRAL FLORIDA
851 North Maitland Avenue
P.O. Box 941508
Maitland, FL 32794-1508
407-682-0555
Hours: Monday through Thursday, 9 to 4; Friday, 9 to 1; first and third Sunday each month, noon to 4. Advance arrangements are recommended.

Founded in 1980 to initiate a program of Holocaust education and raised consciousness, this center moved into its own building six years later. Its growing library now has over 1,500 books, and its archival and documentary materials include films, videotapes, posters, filmstrips, prints, and transparencies.

The multimedia center features teaching programs and its museum has photographs, videos, and a display case containing memorabilia such as Jewish identification cards and prison uniforms.

GEORGIA

❧ DEWS OF HEAVEN ❧

CONGREGATION MICKVE ISRAEL
20 East Gordon Street
Savannah, GA 31401
912-233-1547
Hours: Monday through Friday, 9 to 5 (office). Advance
arrangements are recommended. Tours are conducted by
volunteers, and their hours are slightly unpredictable.

The state of Georgia was named for King George II. Its motto
is "Wisdom, Justice, Moderation" and its capital is Atlanta, but
Savannah is where it all began. James Edward Oglethorpe and 20
other Englishmen set anchor there in July 1733, under a charter
granted by the king. The region seemed a veritable paradise. In the
second boatload of colonists, just five months after the Oglethorpe
landing, were 42 Jews—the largest single group to arrive in North
America during colonial times.

As was true in New Amsterdam, influential Jews in the coloniz-
ing country helped other Jews to colonize Georgia, in an effort to
buffer Carolina from the Spanish and French in the Florida territory.

Three wealthy Sephardic Jews of London, among the richest
men in England, were behind the collection of funds to send poor
members of their religion abroad. Georgia's first Jews were primarily
Spanish and Portuguese of independent means, but there were also
12 indigent German families among them.

The settlers brought with them a Torah and a circumcision box
and probably held religious services in one of their homes during
the first two years.

In July 1735, they formed a synagogue, Congregation Mickve
Israel. Things did not go smoothly, as a letter from a local Christian
minister to a friend in Germany revealed:

*Even the Jews, of whom several families are here already, enjoy all
privileges the same as other colonists [but they] have no Synagogue,*

*which is their own fault; the one element hindering the other in this
regard. The German Jews believe themselves entitled to build a Synagogue and are willing to allow the Spanish Jews to use it with them in
common; the latter, however, reject any such arrangement and demand the preference for themselves.*

The problem became moot, however, by 1742. War between
Spain and England had crossed the Atlantic and a Spanish fleet was
anchored at St. Simon's Island, just off the Georgia coast. The
Sephardim feared for their lives because many of them had professed
Catholicism in order to survive the Inquisition. Having restored
their Judaism, in the eyes of the Catholic church they were guilty of
the crime of apostasy for which punishment was burning at the
stake. The Sephardic Jews hastened to leave Savannah.

The unsettled state of Jews in Savannah continued through the
Revolutionary War. On November 20, 1790, the charter of incorpo-
ration under which the congregation exists today was signed. Their
meeting place remained problematic, however, and their story is
vague. As did other Jewish congregations (see Touro, page 113), they
corresponded with President George Washington and received one
of his loquacious missives:

*To the Hebrew Congregation of the City of Savannah, Georgia. May
the same wonder-working Deity, who long since delivered the Hebrews
from their Egyptian oppressors, planted them in the promised land,
whose providential agency has lately been conspicuous in establishing
these United States as an independent nation, still continue to water
them with the dews of Heaven, and make the inhabitants of every
denomination partake in the temporal and spiritual blessings of that
people, whose God is Jehovah.*

Washington's turn of a phrase was a bit outre, but the sentiment
was what counted.

A small wooden synagogue, built in July 1820, was consumed
by fire in 1829. A new brick building was begun in 1834. In 1878,
expanding again to meet the needs of a growing congregation, the
present building, a tall stone structure with Gothic windows and a
minaretlike dome, was consecrated.

An addition to the back of the building has a room in which
there are three display cases devoted to the history of this synagogue,

which housed one of the six original colonial congregations in America. There are pictures, prayer books, and spice boxes, and there is a community wedding ring, an ornate ring that resembles the very synagogue building in which the Jews of Savannah have worshipped since 1878. It is a historic artifact, but the last time it had been used, I was recently told, was two weeks before.

Highlight: *In one of the three display cases is the Torah brought over from England by the Jews who landed in 1733.*

ILLINOIS

❦ MARC CHAGALL ❧

ART INSTITUTE OF CHICAGO
Michigan Avenue at Adams Street
Chicago, IL 60603
312-443-3600
Hours: Monday, Wednesday, and Friday, 10:30 to 4:30; Tuesday,
10:30 to 8; Saturday, 10 to 5; Sunday and holidays, 12 to 5. Closed
Thursday.

The Chicago Art Institute's 1893 Beaux Arts building was originally part of the World's Columbia Exposition, a fair that celebrated
the city's phoenix-like rise from the ashes of the Great Chicago Fire
of 1871. Today, the Institute has in its collection two important paintings by Marc Chagall, who was born in 1887, between the fire and the
exposition. Chagall is one of the world's greatest Jewish artists. His
work often touched on Jewish life, tradition, and concerns.

Chagall was born in Vitebsk, Russia. His family was orthodox,
and his youth was warm and full with the rituals of Jewish tradition
and ceremony. His father was employed as a fishmonger's assistant.
From his earliest work, Chagall used his hometown as a background
for his art. It returned to him in dreamlike floating imagery.

The young Chagall left Vitebsk to study first in St. Petersburg
and then, in 1910, in Paris. He returned to Russia for a time and then
moved back to Paris. "I was born in Vitebsk, and again in Paris," he
once wrote. His artistic rebirth in Paris occurred during the flourishing of the city's modern art movements—Expressionism, Cubism,
and Fauvism—and Chagall worked in the company of other great
Jewish artists of the "School of Paris": Modigliani, Pascin, and Soutine.
During the German occupation of France, Chagall spent time in
America, but he returned to France after its liberation.

One of the two paintings at the Art Institute, done in 1914, is
called *The Praying Jew (Rabbi of Vitebsk)*. The longer one looks at
this work, the more frightening it becomes. One of the rabbi's eyes

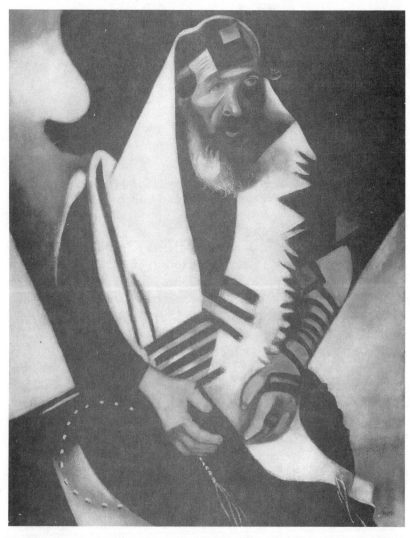

The Praying Jew (Rabbi of Vitebsk) by Marc Chagall, 1914. Courtesy of The Art Institute of Chicago.

White Crucifixion by Marc Chagall, 1938. Gift of Alfred S. Alschuler. Courtesy of The Art Institute of Chicago.

is swollen and seems to have a dark bruise beneath it. Although the background is abstract, it seems ominous, as does a tension that permeates the entire work. Considering that the painting was done during the time of the Russian pogroms, it is not surprising that the subject seems to have an underlay of fear and violence.

Chagall also painted a provocative series of Crucifixions that trouble both Christians and Jews. These show the martyred Christ as a Jew, surrounded by clearly Jewish symbols as well as by references to war and destruction. The Chicago oil, *White Crucifixion*, was done in 1938 and is the earliest of the series. Among the Jewish symbols is Christ's loincloth, which is a tallis (prayer shawl). A Menorah burns, surrounded by a halo, beneath Christ's feet. A Torah scroll in the right-hand corner is on fire, and two lions guarding the Decalogue seem also to be in flames. An army brandishing flags and knives seems to be moving in, and three Jewish men and a woman float, in Chagall's unique, dreamlike imagery, above Christ's head. The face of Christ, whose eyes are closed, is the only image in the painting that has an element of calm, for He has a quiet, detached expression.

The face of Christ in *White Crucifixion* is especially interesting when compared to the intense expression on the face of *The Praying Jew*. Although the emotional contrast is great, there is a notable similarity in their features.

❧ INTERNATIONAL SCOPE ❧

SPERTUS MUSEUM
618 South Michigan Avenue
Chicago, IL 60605
312-922-9012
Hours:　Sunday to Thursday, 10 to 5; Friday, 10 to 3.

When the Chicago College of Jewish Studies opened its doors in the 1920s, it served primarily first-generation immigrants. They were succeeded by American-born children and grandchildren and then by survivors of the Holocaust.

The museum was established in 1968. The seed collection belonged to Maurice Spertus, whose generosity is reflected in both the new name of the school, Spertus College, and the name of the museum. Ceremonial and ritual objects, fine art, textiles, costumes, coins, and medals are found here, and an interesting installation recreates an archaeological dig.

An exceptional Torah ark on display was created by 100 artisans at the Bezalel School in Israel. Sheathed in bronze, two muscular lions guard the steps that lead up to doors that are elaborately embossed.

When I visited this museum, I was impressed by the international and historic span of the objects: cases of Torah scrolls and mantles from Greece, Yemen, and Turkey; a deerskin scroll from Iraq, inside a wooden case that is heavily ornamented in silver and gold; 19th- and 20th-century Sabbath lamps from Libya, made from red pottery painted with black geometric designs; a tiny circumcision coat from Persia, which is, by contrast, elaborate and imperial.

Highlights: *On the second floor, you will find a display case used to exhibit materials from the archives. These exhibits are often local in theme; past topics have been, for example, Chicago's Jewish Clubwomen, Jews in the Civil War, and Chicago's Jewish Architects. This latter subject is particularly interesting in American architecture's premier city.*

Outdoors, in the Julian and Daris Wineberg Sculpture Garden, you will find a 10-foot-high, soaring, curving Flame of Hope by Mexican sculptor Leonardo Nierman. It will be joined by other sculpture in the future.

LOUISIANA

❧ NEW ORLEANS CULTURE ❧

TEMPLE SINAI
6227 St. Charles Avenue
New Orleans, LA 70118
504-861-3693
Hours: Monday through Friday, 9 to 5, and during services on Friday evening and Saturday morning. Call to check times of services.

From Tiffany windows to Chagall prints, this synagogue has beautiful art. Much of the collection was donated by Jacob Weintraub in memory of his wife, Barbara. The Weintraubs escaped to the United States from Nazi Germany and later owned an art gallery in New York City. Many pieces from their personal collection are now housed in the temple's Heller Room. They include particularly interesting and important prints by artists as well known as Chagall, Picasso, Rouault, Jean Arp, Joan Miro, and Louise Nevelson. Not all the artists are Jewish nor do all the works have Judaic significance.

Other artists in the collection are Chaim Gross, Ira Moskowitz, Hyman Bloom, Herman Struck, Shlomo Katz, and Jakob Steinhardt. Their themes often are Jewish. In a ten-part series of lithographs titled *The Jewish Holidays*, Gross integrates Hebrew letters with designs for the holidays. One of Sholom of Safed's lithographs, entitled *Woman of Valor*, illustrates a poem from the book of Proverbs.

The population of New Orleans today numbers 1.3 million; the Jewish community is in the vicinity of 13,000. The first Jew recorded in the city was a merchant and broker named Isaac Monsanto. He brought goods from the West Indies through the port of New Orleans as early as 1758. Monsanto's entry was technically illegal because Louisiana was still under French rule and, according to the Code Noir, Jews were not permitted in French colonies. Monsanto's friendship with the governor helped, at least until 1776, when Spain held Louisiana for a time and both Jews and

Protestants were expelled from New Orleans. The French regained control in 1800 and sold the territory to the United States in 1803. Things were much better after that.

With a few exceptions (they are not, for instance, permitted to join Mardi Gras krews and there has been some ugly Ku Klux Klan activity), Jews have been able to thrive in New Orleans and have become significant leaders and contributors in the community. The Philharmonic Orchestra (now the New Orleans Symphony) and Museum of Art were founded by Jews, and the Jewish merchant princes were great philanthropists (see the next entry).

Temple Sinai, built in 1870, was not the first Jewish house of worship in the city, but it is now the largest, with over 900 families as members. As one of its rabbis once wrote, "One cannot say there is a distinct Jewish culture in New Orleans. Rather there is a distinct New Orleans culture of which the Jewish community is a part."

The current rabbi, Edward Cohn, remarked, when interviewed in *New Orleans* magazine, "You would be hard-pressed to find any-where a Jewish community that has been so accepted, so embraced and treated with such respect as this Jewish community for almost a century and a half."

Highlight: *The sanctuary, with its Tiffany windows and elegant Torah ark surrounded by marble pillars, is extraordinarily beautiful.*

☙ HOUSE AND GARDENS ☞

LONGUE VUE
7 Bamboo Road
New Orleans, LA 70124-1065
504-488-5488
Hours: Tuesday through Saturday, 10 to 4:30; Sunday, 1 to 5.

Down a corridor of live oak trees, their long, slender branches trained to meet in a lacy green ceiling, circuit a small white fountain where the Graces watch the water play, and note, on the frame of the curved wrought-iron doors leading into the circular vestibule, a small silver mezuzah—the sign that a Jewish family lives within, or once did.

Edgar Bloom Stern was born in New Orleans in 1886, and Edith Rosenwald Stern was born in Chicago in 1895. He was successful in many enterprises, starting in his family's cotton business and moving on to banking, lumber, oil, publishing, real estate, radio, and television. Her father made his fortune in Sears, Roebuck & Company. She had had a brief first marriage before she and Edgar met, and it's said they fell in love at first sight.

Edgar Stern proposed marriage to Edith Rosenwald one afternoon when they stopped for tea at an inn on the Hudson River. The name of the inn was the name they would later give their manse— Longue Vue. The marriage ceremony was held on a private train en route to Illinois, and the wedding reception was held at the Rosenwald estate just outside Chicago. After a honeymoon in Europe, the couple settled down to the serious business of married life in New Orleans.

If their long view that day on the Hudson could have scoped the future, they would have seen a life of prosperity, comfort, and good works. He was a Republican and she a Democrat, but they saw eye-to-eye on the subject of philanthropy. Each of them, independently, was awarded a Loving Cup from The New Orleans Times-Picayune in recognition of their charitable endeavors. He received his award in 1930 and she was given hers in 1964, five years after her husband's death. She survived him by nearly 20 years. One of her final gestures was to leave her residence as a gift, having expressed the wish "that my house and garden will serve some public use, the garden as presently used for horticultural functions and exhibitions and the house as a museum of decorative arts."

Not many house museums were built as late as this one, which the Sterns moved into in December, 1942. It has been kept as it was during their life there, and serves as an exemplar of a wealthy, fashionable life-style of the era.

My overriding impression after I visited Longue Vue was that it was a little crazy. Maybe it was the chintz, the flowery wallpaper, and the patterned rugs, all of which seemed to be battling for attention. The painted furniture (a bit of chinoiserie here and there) and an awful reproduction of an abstract painting by Wassily Kandinsky (the original was donated to the art museum), in a room paneled in dark blue, draped in patterned gold, and centering on a flowery gold rug atop a blue carpet didn't help.

Mr. Stern's dressing room gave me particular pause. The wallpaper was faux marble, black and green, and there were terazzo floors and mirrored wall panels, all very shiny.

I was charmed by the room devoted to flower arranging, which had deep sinks and flower prints on the walls. And I was awestruck by the fact that one small room was entirely devoted to *wrapping presents!*

The point is, these were real people. They didn't live in a mausoleum. Their tastes were boisterous, or, at the very least, eclectic. They bought what they liked and answered to no one.

In one section of the main hall, there's a trestle table that has identical wood-back chairs placed against the wall at either end, identical pitchers facing each other on the table top, and a ceramic bowl with two birds (facing each other) in between the pitchers. Two wall sconces, each with two candles, are at either side of a picture that is above the very center of the table.

It's pairs all the way: beyond two white Doric columns are two convex mirrors surmounted by two brass eagles, next to a door that has twin plant stands and plants on either side, under another set of two-candle wall sconces.

Didn't everybody's mother decorate like that?

I suspect that their own clear-headed purposefulness allowed the Sterns to live sanely in such aesthetic turmoil.

Edith Stern collected a kind of ceramic called Creamware. It was developed by Josiah Wedgewood in 1763, and was made by other English potteries as well as his. Plates, baskets, and all manner of pitchers and decorative items for the home are in the Stern collection of this earthenware, which may be the largest in the country.

The architecture of Longue Vue is a putative classical revival style, although the front and the back don't exactly match. The gardens were Edith Stern's passion. I remember with particular pleasure the camellias and the yellow garden, outside the guest cottage (the Whim House). She designed the yellow garden herself (yellow was her favorite color). Only plants with yellow flowers or yellow variegated foliage were grown there: Gold Mound, Rain of Gold, Gold Spot euonymus, butterfly vine, Carolina yellow jessamine, daffodils, narcissi, yellow callas, yellow pansies, calendula, yellow hibiscus, chrysanthemums, and yellow Lady Banks roses.

Let me try to describe the Art Gallery, originally a porch but closed in first as an oak and chintz-filled sunroom and later transformed to show Mrs. Stern's contemporary art collection. It has two tufted, S-curved, plush, yellow-silk-upholstered loveseats that are fringed along the bottom. They stand on a very shiny black floor. The walls are hung with abstract canvases; one wall has a floor-to-ceiling series of squares in shades from black to white. On either side of that, beneath two smaller, colorful canvases with geometric shapes, are two outrageous rococo gilt chairs. Is that not to smile?

Highlight: *In a small room called the Upper Gallery, the family history is on display via photographs and memorabilia. There are not any other specifically Jewish objects in the collection, beyond the mezuzah at the front door. You will probably notice, as many visitors do, that the mezuzah is on the wrong side of that doorway: it is on the left rather than the right. When guides are asked about the discrepancy, they can only shrug their shoulders and say, "I don't know. The rabbi did it."*

MISSISSIPPI

❧ DOWN HOME ☙

THE MUSEUM OF SOUTHERN JEWISH LIFE
Henry Jacobs Camp
Utica, MS
Mailing address: P. O. Box 16528
Jackson, MS 39236-6042
601-362-6357
Hours: Call or write to schedule a visit.

The story told at this museum begins about 200 years ago. Confronted with the sweatshops and smokestacks of the industrial Northeast, Jewish immigrant families sought refuge anew, this time in the green hills and fertile bottomlands of the deep South. They worked on farms and in shops, and they went from town to town peddling everything from clothing to kitchenware.

Thus did Jews settle in and become Southern Jews. Some anglicized their names, from Goldsmith to Gold, Rosenzwig to Rose, Applebaum to Apple, for instance. But they established synagogues and cemeteries and carried on the traditions of their religious faith. As time passed, members of the younger generations moved to metropolitan centers, leaving behind the small rural enclaves and synagogues their families had built.

In 1986, a group of Tennesseans began making forays into areas such as Rapides Parish, Louisiana; Port Gibson, Mississippi; and Helena, Arkansas, where Jewish communities had once been active. They had a sense both of commitment and of racing against time: the landmarks and the people with any memories of life in those communities were fast vanishing. A cultural preservation mission was launched; its goal was to find and save artifacts and whatever could be salvaged from abandoned synagogues. They also sought personal memorabilia: family photographs, correspondence, memoirs, and Judaica.

With the help of a grant from the Plough Foundation of Memphis, a museum was built on the grounds of the Henry Jacobs Camp, southwest of Jackson, Mississippi. The camp itself had been a project of Reform congregations of Mississippi, Arkansas, Louisiana, and Tennessee. Mainly a summer camp, in addition to recreational activities, it helps young people to understand the breadth of Judaism. For older campers, there is an eight-week stay modeled after an Israeli kibbutz.

The museum has already accumulated a collection of religious artifacts—stained glass windows, seder plates, menorahs, and salvaged architectural details—and a wonderful photograph collection, not only of former times, but also of Jews today.

The contemporary photos came from excursions made by the museum's project director, Vicki Reikes Fox, and photographer Bill Aron. They traveled around the South and found these images, among many others, representing what is both Southern and Jewish:

- A road sign from Louisiana that reads "KAPLAN." The town was named after Abram Kaplan, a Jewish immigrant who settled there in 1850.

- An absolutely down-home shot of a man and his wife seated on porch steps. They are Cliff and Wilma Abrams, in front of their Brookhaven, Mississippi, home. Cliff Abrams was born in that house 85 years before the picture was taken.

- A farming couple, Benji and Betty Lee Lamensdorf of Cary, Mississippi, standing in a large expanse of waving green vegetation. They grow cotton, wheat, and pecans, and own one of the largest cotton gins in the South.

This collection tells a story of "Menorahs and Magnolias," the headline used for an article in a local paper. It is also a story of Southern pride and Jewish determination and of Jewish pride and Southern determination.

Highlight: *Bill Aron's photograph of Joe Martin Eber and Meyer Gilman says more than one could imagine about the texture of one corner of Southern Judaism.*

One man is probably in his sixties or seventies, the other perhaps thirty. Both are casually dressed, the older man in a plaid shirt, the younger in short sleeves and wearing a baseball cap. The cap's insignia is that of the U. S. Postal Service. They look as though they might be at a cookout, but each man wears a tallis and each holds an elaborately covered Torah.

MISSOURI

❧ WINDOWS ❧

TEMPLE B'NAI JEHUDAH
712 East 69th Street
Kansas City, MO 64131
816-363-1050
Hours: By appointment.

Louis Comfort Tiffany usually gets credit for it but John La Farge actually discovered and patented a new development in opalescent glass, in 1880. La Farge thus launched the revival of interest in stained glass in America. (Tiffany's patent was not issued until 1881.) La Farge, born in Brooklyn, studied art in Europe during the time when the medieval glass tradition was being revived in England. Returning to America, he began experimenting with designs. His first major commission was for Trinity Church in Boston, designed by the renowned Boston architect Henry Hobson Richardson.

In 1907, three years before his death, La Farge received a commission for 20 windows (10 large and 10 small) for the first Temple B'nai Jehudah in Kansas City, Missouri. Some of the smaller windows were later disassembled for use in repairs and one was given to a Kansas City hospital for its chapel, but the rest remain and are viewed as the jewels of the current synagogue's collection. They represent the only windows La Farge is known to have made for a Jewish house of worship.

The theme is historical: 10 periods in Jewish history are represented, from ancient times to the beginning of the 20th century. The first window, for example, represents the Age of the Patriarchs. The upper portion shows a burning altar and the Hebrew inscription "God, the Almighty." In the center of the lower window is the phrase "Surely the Lord is in this place."

The La Farge windows are in the halls and rotunda of the temple, which also house an unusually fine collection of art and ceremonial objects. There are display cases in the front hall and other sculptures and paintings appear throughout the building. This is the largest public collection of Judaica in Kansas City. With 1,800 families, Temple B'nai Jehudah is one of the largest Reform congregations in the United States.

Highlights: *In this collection are a large number of paintings and prints by a wide range of Israeli and Jewish artists. A particular favorite is a series of silk screens by Seelig, an Israeli artist. The subject of the suite is the seven days of creation.*

NEBRASKA

❧ CORRIDOR CASES ☙

NEBRASKA JEWISH HISTORICAL SOCIETY
Omaha Jewish Community Center
333 South 132nd Street
Omaha, NE 68154
402-334-8200, ext. 277
Hours: Historical Society: Monday through Thursday, 9 to 5. JCC
building: Monday through Thursday, 8 A.M. to 10 P.M.; Friday,
8 A.M. to 5 P.M.; Saturday and Sunday, 8:30 A.M. to 7 P.M.

Omaha is the largest city in Nebraska. The site was occupied by
Omaha Indians until a treaty opened the Nebraska Territory to
settlement in 1854. About that time, the first Jews arrived; they
established their first congregation in 1871.

Although the Jewish population of Omaha numbers fewer than
10,000 out of a total greater-metropolitan population of about
570,000, it is an active and involved population.

In the JCC, a Corridor of History is made up of four glass cases
and six large wall panels. There are two or three exhibits every year
on subjects such as World Wars I and II, sports, political life, Omaha
in 1948, the Holocaust, and early synagogues.

NORTH CAROLINA

❧ KANOF COLLECTION ❧

NORTH CAROLINA MUSEUM OF ART
2110 Blue Ridge Boulevard
Raleigh, NC 27607
919-833-1935
Hours: Tuesday through Saturday, 9 to 5; Friday, 9 to 9; Sunday, noon to 5; closed Monday.

The North Carolina Museum of Art is unique in the United States: it is the only general art museum with a permanent gallery devoted to Judaica. Before the Royal Ontario Museum opened its Judaica gallery in 1989, North Carolina was unique in all of North America.

Neither the state nor the city of Raleigh has an especially large or unusual Jewish population. How is it, then, that this handsome installation of both old and new Judaica of the highest quality is located here?

The answer comes in two parts.

First, this is an innovative institution. Its collection belongs to the state which, in 1947, appropriated $1 million for the purchase of works of art. Representative John Kerr, whose inspired oratory persuaded his colleagues in the state legislature to do "the far-sighted, statesmanlike thing without being afraid," said, in 1947, "Mr. Speaker, I know that I am facing a hostile audience, but man cannot live by bread alone." The appropriation made North Carolina the first state in the nation to buy art for its citizens. Anyone who followed the headlining news of the art world during 1990 will be justifiably stunned to learn this fact about North Carolina. Jesse Helms, ardent protagonist of the National Endowment for the Arts and considered no friend of art at all, is North Carolina's senator, elected many times over. (The moral of this story is, don't judge a state by its senator.)

Second, North Carolina had Abram Kanof. This part of the North Carolina equation is ultimately less of a dichotomy, for

Dr. Kanof is a world renowned collector, connoisseur, and writer on Judaica. He is also a pediatrician and medical researcher of no small accomplishment and reputation. Born in Russia in 1903 and raised in New York City, he and his wife, Frances, a dermatologist, both loved and collected art. Dr. Abram Kanof was named organizing chairman of New York's Jewish Museum when it was in its planning stages. In 1950, the Kanofs founded the Tobe Pascher Workshop, a school for contemporary craftsmanship of Judaica, at the Jewish Museum. The Workshop, another first in this country, is superseded worldwide only by the Bezalel School of Israel.

The doctors Kanof moved to Raleigh to live near their daughter, who is also a physician, in the 1970s. In 1975, Ceremonial Art in the Judaic Tradition, an exhibition organized by Dr. Abram Kanof, drew an enormous audience, far exceeding the anticipated number of visitors and selling out the show's catalog.

The astute museum administration began, under Kanof's guidance, to build a collection of Judaica. The museum was in cramped quarters at the time, and it was not until a new building was completed that room could be set aside for the Judaica Gallery, funds for which were donated by the Kanofs. On December 18, 1983, the Judaica Gallery opened at the new North Carolina Museum of Art, setting a precedent in an unexpected venue.

Among the 35 to 40 objects in the gallery is a highly ornamental silver and gilt cup. Made in Germany during the second half of the 19th century, the cup was for the prophet Elijah. During the Passover meal, which celebrates the release of the Israelites from bondage in Egypt, a cup is always filled to the brim with wine. Often, the front door of the home is left open so that Elijah can enter, and some adults have been known to spill a bit of wine from the cup to signify that Elijah has indeed visited the house.

A beautiful, vividly colored ketubah has a picture of a bride and groom surrounded by vines and floral patterns. Circumcision instruments are among the most carefully ornamented Judaica. In the Raleigh set, the handle of the scalpel illustrates Abraham offering his son Isaac as a sacrifice to the Lord. Moses holding the Tablets of the Law is on the handle of the probe, and, on the flacon of styptic powder, a worried mother stands in the background overseeing the circumcision of her son.

Contrasting with the highly ornamental pieces in the collection are some contemporary designs, such as a small silver mezuzah by Ludwig Wolpert, often called the founder of modern Jewish ceremonial art. He was a participant in the Tobe Pascher Workshop, in New York. This mezuzah, with elongated Hebrew lettering forming its design, was presented to the collection by the artist himself, in honor of the Kanofs' fiftieth wedding anniversary.

One of the joyful silver pieces in the collection is a scene of King David dancing before the Ark of the Covenant, which is carried by four robed men and topped by two angels. Their robes fall about their bodies to reveal the movement of their arms and legs. David, carrying his lyre, is hopping energetically. The small scene is full of animation. Dr. Kanof told me he had bought it in the 1950s in "a store on Fifth Avenue and 59th Street in New York." It had been "appropriated" from the Czar after the Russian Revolution, as far as Dr. Kanof knew.

Perhaps the most important work that the Kanofs presented to the museum is a seder plate made by Ilya Schor, an Eastern European Jew who immigrated to the United States. Schor's signature was accompanied by his artistic symbol, a dove in flight. His work retains a somewhat old European style, and the detail and craftsmanship of his pieces are skillful beyond compare. He was inspired by the Bible and Jewish folklore and life in the shtetl.

Sadly, Schor's work did not receive the recognition it deserved during his lifetime (he died in 1961), but it has since become highly prized and sought after.

Highlight: *Besides its luminous history, this museum has a fine collection of art. In a stark modern building designed by Edward Durell Stone and dedicated in 1983, visitors find a dramatic setting as soon as they walk into the entrance lobby. Juxtaposed there are figures from ancient Egypt and abstract art of the 20th century, representing the time span of the collection.*

Attributed to Anton Eisenhoit (German, active c. 1650–1700). *David Dancing Before the Ark of the Covenant.* North Carolina Museum of Art, Raleigh, Gift of Abram and Frances Pascher Kanof.

Austrian, mid-19th century. Esther scroll. North Carolina Museum of Art, Gift of Abram and Frances Pascher Kanof.

OHIO

⮜ HEADS UP! ⮞

CINCINNATI ART MUSEUM
Eden Park
Cincinnati, OH 45202-1596
513-721-5204
Hours: Tuesday, Thursday, Friday, Saturday, 10 to 5; Wednesday,
10 to 9; Sunday, noon to 5.

If you have already discovered Moses Jacob Ezekiel at the Hebrew Union College collection (see page 157), you may want to see more of his sculpture. If you first see his work here, be sure to put Hebrew Union College on your itinerary.

The Cincinnati Art Museum has a number of his works. Among them are *Ecce Homo*, a 21-inch-tall bust of Jesus Christ crowned with thorns; four marble portrait busts, including *Henry Wadsworth Longfellow*; and a marble torso of *Judith*. The latter is cut off several inches below the waist and curiously draped to leave one shoulder and breast bare. The skirt is oddly laced at the waist. Judith's hair is in tight curls and she has a look of grim determination on her face.

Another important image of Judith in this museum is *Judith with the Head of Holofernes*, done by Botticelli in about 1468. On this small canvas (a bit larger than 11 by 8 inches), Judith is accompanied by her maid. If Ezekiel's sculpture shows Judith resigned and courageous, probably before the deed was done, Botticelli's picture shows her afterward. The still turbaned head of Holofernes is in a basket that the maid is carrying, almost nonchalantly, balanced atop her head. Judith is striding forward, her curved sword in one hand and a delicate olive branch in the other. The courageous expression of the sculpture has been replaced by a more equivocal, almost wistful gaze—not the expected expression of someone who has just decapitated the enemy. This oil sketch is an earlier version of the Botticelli painting of Judith that is in the Uffizi museum in Florence.

On the subject of decapitations, Cincinnati also owns a painting by Bernardo Strozzi, from about 1620–1630, of *David with the*

Head of Goliath. David has a few jaunty plumes in his hat and a quite delighted expression on his face. He, too, is holding a sword in one hand, but in his other hand is a bunch of hair by which he is holding Goliath's enormous head. No ambiguity or regretfulness shows in David; bravado is more the order of his day.

One might hesitate to say that a theme runs through the Old Testament works at Cincinnati's museum, but it is curious that yet a fourth important work in the collection is Peter Paul Rubens' oil sketch of *Samson and Delilah.* At least she indulged only in barbering, not in decapitation.

Highlight: *An imminent act of violence — and a supreme moment of truth — gets an almost environmental treatment in the painting* Landscape with the Offering of Isaac, *by Henri met de Bles, a Flemish artist of the first part of the 16th century. More about landscape than about Abraham's sacrifice, the painting shows a gorgeous, hilly vista with a city in the distance.*

❧ THE PRESERVATION TRAIL ❧

HILLEL JEWISH STUDENT CENTER AT THE UNIVERSITY OF CINCINNATI
Rose Warner House
2615 Clifton Avenue
Cincinnati, OH 45220-2885
513-221-6728
Hours: Monday through Friday, 9 to 5.

On Friday, June 30, 1989, a picture of Rabbi Abie I. Ingber appeared, in full color, on the front page of *The Cincinnati Enquirer.* He was wearing a purple shirt, pushed up to the elbows, and a bright yellow hardhat. He looked and *was* very happy. The rabbi had reason to celebrate. He had just discovered the oldest existing synagogue standing west of the Allegheny Mountains. He found it in the walls of a vacant building after having read about its existence in a 129-year-old magazine.

"Holy mackerel, this is unbelievable!" he is reported to have said. When a rabbi says "holy mackerel," you know he's surprised.

Abie Ingber is one of those enthusiasts whose energy and commitment leap off pages. He has a self-imposed mission of saving synagogue artifacts. He is a graduate of Cincinnati's Hebrew Union College and the son of Polish parents who survived the Holocaust. Now in his early 40s, he has been on the preservation trail since 1977.

His searching began when Rabbi Ingber organized a group of University of Cincinnati B'nai B'rith Hillel Foundation students to clean up a neglected Jewish cemetery that had fallen into disrepair. Returning to the cemetery the following week, his attention was drawn to a window in an old church a block north of the cemetery. The section was slated for urban renewal. The window was not a church window; it was a circular stained-glass window with a Jewish star. Inside the star was the word Zion.

Ingber learned that the building had once been the Ansche Sholom Synagogue, a small Orthodox synagogue known affectionately as the "Roumainische Shul." The congregation had been founded in 1902 in a part of Cincinnati that was full of immigrants at the turn of the century. Jews moved out of the area in 1932 and the building was abandoned by the congregation. With permission of the city, the window was removed, professionally cleaned, reframed, and installed in the main entrance to the Hillel building.

Another stained-glass window that came to Hillel through Ingber's efforts had been in the second house of worship used by Cincinnati's first Jewish congregation. This window had already been salvaged from a demolished building and one of Ingber's widening circle of preservation contacts had seen it advertised in the classified section of a newspaper.

From former synagogues in northern Kentucky, he has retrieved lions that once guarded a Torah ark, and a six-foot memorial tablet. A ceremony at Hillel to rededicate Judaica from a vanished Newport, Kentucky, congregation brought 100 current and former residents of the town to honor their roots. In reciting the mourners' kaddish, a prayer said with congregational responses, many were moved to tears.

The business of salvation can be emotional. Rabbi Ingber recounted how, black with soot, he climbed down from the attic crawl space of a former temple with a handmade, green corduroy Torah cover in his hand. Tears welled up in the eyes of the student who

was with him. "I remember coming to this synagogue with my father. And now all that's left are a few tattered tallisim and rat-eaten
tefillin straps." Most of the ritual items from that excursion were
beyond saving and were buried in a Jewish cemetery. The Torah
cover is now in the Hillel collection.

One day, a woman from St. Louis called to say she had some ark
lions. They had been given to her husband, an exterminator, by a
client who had stored them in an attic. The synagogue from which
they had come had been demolished long before. When he learned
that a member of the Hillel board was about to make a business trip
to St. Louis, the rabbi asked, "Can you pick up something for me?
Two lions?" They, too, were somewhat the worse for wear, but they
have been lovingly restored and are now in what has been affectionately named the Lion's Den at Hillel.

Part of Ingber's efforts are for the purpose of simple, honorable
preservation, but he described other goals:

*I like to think that the artifacts make our Hillel building a little more
heymish. I hope that the collection of stained-glass windows and other
synagogue relics reminds our students of their hometown synagogues
and shows the Jewish community the importance of preserving our
architectural heritage. . . . Walking away from a synagogue and
leaving the Judaica is like leaving the soul of the building behind.*

Recognition of his efforts has brought the rabbi several awards
and, somewhat unusual, an annotation in the American Automobile
Association's *AAA Tourbook.* It is the only Hillel mentioned in
AAA's and probably anyone else's general guidebook. "Visiting parents are also impressed with our contemporary facility and historic
Judaica," Ingber reports. "They feel that if Hillel takes such good care
of 100-year-old objects their 18-year-olds will be in good hands."

Highlight: *The lions in Hillel's den reveal the enormous diversity
of those ark guardians, some of which look fierce while others are
funny, foolish, or simply charming. A pair of hand-carved, gold-
painted lions from the now defunct United Hebrew Congregation of
Newport, Kentucky, have red glass eyes and almost comical surprised
expressions on their faces.*

A VERY PRETTY CITY

SKIRBALL MUSEUM CINCINNATI BRANCH
Hebrew Union College, Jewish Institute of Religion
3101 Clifton Avenue
Cincinnati, OH 45220-2488
513-221-1875
Hours: Monday through Friday, 11 to 4; Sunday, 2 to 4.

General Arthur St. Clair, Governor of the Northwest Territories, had a reason for changing the name of Losantiville to Cincinnati in 1789. St. Clair was among the founders of the Society of Cincinnati, an elite association of male descendants of officers who served in the regular Continental Army or Navy during the American Revolution. The organization's first president was none other than George Washington.

Washington was often compared to the Society's namesake, the Roman general Cincinnatus, who was admired particularly because he had laid down his plough only long enough to rescue Rome, and then went back to farming. The implication is that, like Cincinnatus, Washington, who resigned both his military commission and the presidency after two terms, had no taste for power.

Cincinnati's boosters included Henry Wadsworth Longfellow ("Queen City of the West," he called it) and Charles Dickens, who ranked Cincinnati just after Boston for being pretty. Hills, the Ohio River, parks, more trees per capita than perhaps any other American city, a famous zoo, and good museums, including the one at Hebrew Union College, all add up to recommend Cincinnati for a visit.

The Hebrew Union College here is the original seminary for the emerging Reform movement. Founded in 1875, it was the first seminary in America established for training Reform rabbis, and it is a leading institution for Jewish scholarship. Colleges with the same name in New York, Los Angeles, and Jerusalem followed many years later. Museum headquarters, however, are at the Skirball Museum in Los Angeles (page 198), where the major part of the shared collection is housed.

Cincinnati's campus does not lack for things to see and learn. On the contrary: the American Jewish Archives are here, with thousands of memoirs, letters, wills, and unpublished papers dating back to 1654, plus congregational and genealogical records, and historic documents. The Klau Library and Dalsheimer Rare Book Building have 15th-century Hebrew and non-Hebrew books of Jewish interest—one of the foremost collections of its kind. There are also scrolls, a stamp collection significant to Jewish life and history, an outstanding collection of broadsides and bookplates, and a major Spinoza collection. (Advance notice of two weeks is required to see these collections.)

Although part of Skirball, the museum's exhibition schedule is autonomous. The museum originated a show of the works of Moses Jacob Ezekiel, who, though born in Richmond in 1844, moved to Cincinnati in 1868, giving the city claim to him as part of its artistic heritage. For his 1873 sculpture *Israel*, Ezekiel won the prestigious Prix de Rome awarded by the Berlin Royal Academy of Art. He was the first American to be so honored. Ezekiel moved to Italy when his work started to get rave reviews. He lived on the outskirts of Rome and his studio became a salon and showplace where the elite gathered.

The Ezekiel exhibit was dismantled years ago, but the great prize, the Prix de Rome, *Israel*, remains in HUC's Cincinnati museum. There are also fabulous collections of mizrah and ketubot, and an exceptional baroque silver Hanukkah lamp, in the shape of a temple, from 19th-century Hungary. A bit more subtle in its magnetism is the *Genesis* plaque, designed and executed as a cornerstone of the 1955 Procter & Gamble building in Cincinnati—the first line from Genesis is written in 43 languages. The plaque was produced by the famous Rookwood Pottery company.

Recent expansion of a campus building called Meyerson Hall gave the museum new space for its permanent exhibit and a special gallery to feature works by prominent Jewish artists. On the third floor is a Torah section; another space is devoted to American Jewish history, particularly the Jewish presence in Cincinnati. The mezzanine has a Discovery Room and arts center for children.

Highlight: *Established in Cincinnati in 1880, Rookwood Pottery was one of America's great manufacturers of arts and crafts products. Rookwood closed in 1955, but among the marvelous objects produced there you will discover a most unusual set of bookends. Looking rather like the entrance of a castle fortress with crenelated towers, these bookends represent one of the Hebrew Union College's classroom buildings.*

❧ FABRIC OF JUDAISM ☙

THE TEMPLE MUSEUM OF RELIGIOUS ART
University Circle at Silver Park
Cleveland, Ohio 44106
216-791-7755
Hours: By appointment.

There are 30 synagogues and about 65,000 Jews in the Greater Cleveland area. One of the most beautiful synagogues is Temple Tifereth (Glory of) Israel, a National Landmark building of golden domes and arched windows and doors. It was built in 1924 for a congregation that had been formed in 1850.

In 1950, to commemorate the 100th anniversary of the congregation, a museum was dedicated. For decades, members of the congregation have been collecting Judaica; now, more than forty years later, they have one of the most significant collections in the country. One member presented the museum with a Persian vessel for water or oil, which dates back to 2000 B.C.E. There are also Torah scrolls from Czechoslovakia, which were hidden from the Nazis during the War; antique silver Torah ornaments; folk art objects from many countries; sculptures, paintings, and lithographs by well-known artists (Lipchitz and Kaufmann, for example); and a collection of pieces from the Bezalel School.

The extraordinary category of the collection here is fabric: ark curtains and valances, covers for a reader's desk, Torah mantles and binders, and many other exquisite pieces. The use of cloth for Jewish ritual is stated in the Bible: "Thou shalt make the tabernacle with ten curtains of fine twined linen, and blue, and purple, and scarlet; with the cherubims of cunning work shalt thou make them." So did the Lord instruct the Children of Israel through Moses.

The Temple Museum's permanent collection boasts forty prime examples of ritual cloths. Many of these articles came into the United States under the auspices of the Jewish Cultural Reconstruction Foundation, the agency that dispersed objects found in Europe after the Holocaust.

One piece struck a personal chord, although it isn't among the most notable for rarity or workmanship. It is a 19th-century scarf painted with an outdoor scene in which hundreds of German Jewish soldiers are standing around an altar, prayer books in hand, observing Yom Kippur in an army camp at Metz.

Highlight: *Fabrics cannot be kept on exhibit for prolonged periods, so it is difficult to predict what rare treasures will be displayed at any future time. The museum owns some 17th-century ark curtains and valances that are among the best in the country. Particularly beautiful is one set embroidered with silver and gold thread on a burgundy velvet background. The two guardian lions are incongruously poised on the tips of pointed leaves, atop decorative columns that flank a candelabra and Decalogue.*

❧ PRINTZESS ☙

WESTERN RESERVE HISTORICAL SOCIETY LIBRARY
10825 East Boulevard
Cleveland, OH 44106
216-721-5722
Hours: Tuesday through Saturday, 9 to 5.

Seeking to escape induction into the Russian army, Max Sandin, who was born in Russia, immigrated to the United States in 1910 and arrived in Cleveland in November of that year. He worked as a peddler for a brief time and then obtained employment as a painter and paper hanger, becoming a member of a local union. Sandin was a conscientious objector during both world wars. Drafted during World War I, his noncompliance with orders resulted in a death sentence, which was later commuted by President Woodrow Wilson to a term in prison. Eventually pardoned from that sentence, Max Sandin continued his involvement in anti-war activities. He was associated with the American Civil Liberties Union, the War Resisters League, and the Fellowship of Reconciliation.

This brief synopsis of an eventful life is found in *A Guide to Jewish History Sources in the History Library of the Western Reserve Historical Society*, published in 1983. In what should ostensibly be a

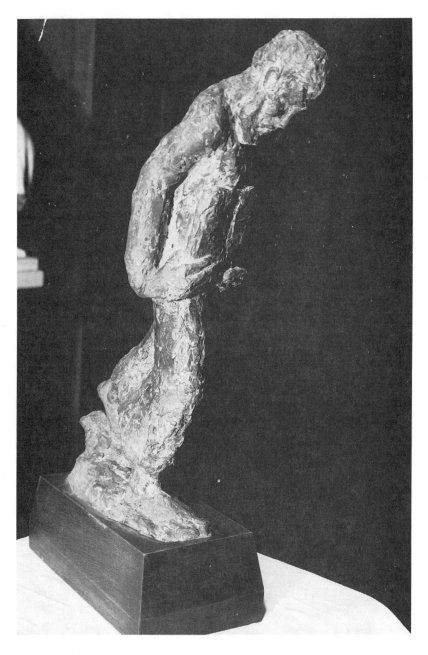

Moses—Descent from the Mountain by Katherine H. Bercovici, 1960.
Courtesy of The Temple Museum of Religious Art, Cleveland, Ohio.

The Limoges 19th-century Seder plate has the order of the service inscribed, in Hebrew, around the border. Courtesy of The Temple Museum of Religious Art, Cleveland, Ohio.

dry archival record of the collection, you find instead allusions to great, promising dramas.

Even the plain brown paper cover of the catalog, with just a square of Hebrew text for decoration, has unusual significance. The text is from an opening page of the ethical testament given to emigrants who left Unsleben, Bavaria, for Cleveland on 21 Iyar 5599 (May 5, 1839). The text reads, "May God send His angel before you/ May no ill befall you/ In all your ways know Him/ and He will make your paths straight." The manuscript from which it is taken is the oldest in Cleveland's Jewish Archives.

Sandin's papers fill a single archival container (five linear feet of space), which also holds his autobiography, *I Was Sentenced to be Shot*, as well as correspondence, legal documents, and other miscellaneous materials concerning his childhood in the Russian shtetl where he was born in 1889, his immigration to the United States, and his activities until his death in 1967.

Henry Spira, who came from Hungary to central Ohio in 1879, also worked as a peddler but, after some time in the wholesale liquor business, he established a foreign exchange and banking office that included a steamship ticket agency. The Bank of Henry Spira, later known as the Spira Savings and Loan Association, served many immigrants.

The Printz-Biederman company's records, from 1914 to 1957, tell about a business that specialized in the manufacture of women's coats marketed under the trademark Printzess. By 1934, the company was a large concern on Printzess Square in Cleveland. Operations ceased in 1979. Among the archival material is documentation of the efforts of the International Ladies' Garment Workers' Union to organize this very paternalistic company during the 1930s.

The Jewish Bakers' Union, Local 56, was active in Cleveland from 1924 to 1950, and its records are here. The photographs in the collection include portraits and views of the Sherwin Baking Company, from around 1930 to 1960: members of the family, interior and exterior shots of the bakery, and pictures of the patriotic window displays arranged by the company during World War II.

From time to time, the Western Reserve Historical Society assembles exhibits such as Founders: Cleveland's Jewish Community Before the Civil War, which was shown in 1990.

Highlight: *The Society library, in which the Jewish History Archives are kept, is in a new, low, red brick building (close by the History Museum and the Crawford Auto–Aviation Museum). The most outstanding architectural feature of the building is a beautiful arched window at the north end of the three-story reading room. It was originally the doorway to a building that stood on Cleveland's Public Square from 1892 to 1982. The building was designed by the leading architectural firm of D. H. Burnham & Company, which was headquartered in Chicago.*

OKLAHOMA

↜ TULSY TOWN ↞

GERSHON & REBECCA FENSTER MUSEUM OF JEWISH ART
1223 East 17th Place
Tulsa, Oklahoma 74120
918-582-3732
Hours: Tuesday through Friday, 10 to 4; Sunday, 1 to 4. Advance arrangements are recommended.

In the 1830s, Creek Indians moved from Alabama to an area along the Arkansas River named Tulsey Town. In 1901, oil was discovered in Tulsey Town, and the area, which is today the city of Tulsa, became known as the Oil Capital of the World. Now a transportation and banking center as well, Tulsa's population is close to 700,000. The first Jewish Congregation in Oklahoma was formed in 1903, in Oklahoma City.

The Fenster Gallery, located at the B'nai Emunah Synagogue, was founded in 1966 to express an appreciation of ritual and ceremonial objects used in the synagogue. The collection also includes objects for holiday and life-cycle events, historical artifacts, costumes, archaeological objects, and materials that relate the story of anti-Semitism and the Holocaust. Trained docents give tours.

Highlight: *A beautiful groom's marriage vest of gold embroidery on red satin was made in Cochin, India, during the 18th century.*

SOUTH CAROLINA

❧ RICE AND INDIGO ❧

KAHAL KADOSH BETH ELOHIM MUSEUM
Administration Building (behind the Temple)
86 Hasell Street
Charleston, SC 29401
803-723-1090
Hours: Monday through Friday, 9 to 3.

One *could* write a history of Charleston, South Carolina, and leave the Jews out. Charlestonians will tell anyone that the city is located where the Ashley and Cooper rivers meet and form the Atlantic Ocean. In the Carolina Low Country, first settled in 1670, its name was originally Charles Town. Rice was the first crop to bring wealth to the region; later, marketable indigo brought great prosperity. They were complementary crops: rice grew in the swamplands and was cultivated and tended during the winter, and indigo flourished in high, dry soil and was cared for during the summer.

Charles Town was the most exciting and bustling southern metropolis of the pre-Revolution era, and the only large urban center south of Philadelphia. By the time of the Revolutionary War, its population was around 12,000. It was a seat of provincial justice, a hub of commerce, and a showcase of splendor and style. As travelers of the era remarked, Charles Town enjoyed "opulence and beauty," and its genteel population "are Exceedingly civil and kind to strangers."

A standard history book may ignore the fact, but it has been recorded that the earliest known reference to a Jew in the English settlement of Charles Town was in 1695. The man's name is unknown, but he was mentioned by the colony's Governor John Archdale, who said he had a Spanish-speaking Jew as an interpreter in dealing with captive Florida Indians who spoke Spanish.

That was before the area's growth began. By 1749, when the halcyon days had started, there was a large enough Jewish community to form the Kahal Kadosh Beth Elohim (Holy Congregation House of God), and one of its members, Moses Lindo, helped to develop the indigo crop that gave such benefit to the town.

At first, prayers were said in private homes; in 1775, they were offered in an improvised synagogue. Not until after the Revolutionary War, in 1792, was construction begun of what was to be the largest and most impressive synagogue in the country. When the Marquis de Lafayette saw it after its completion, he proclaimed it "spacious and elegant." This fine two-story building had a pitched roof, arched windows, and what looks like a spire, although there appear to have been two copper balls along its shaft and a decoration resembling a fleur de lis at the top.

There were nearly 600 Jews living in Charles Town when Solomon N. Carvalho was born there in 1815. Most of these Jews were of Spanish-Portugese descent, as was Carvalho. He probably studied art at the Jewish academy founded in Charles Town by Isaac Harby. It is known that he moved, with his family, to Baltimore in 1828, ten years before the synagogue was destroyed in the great Charleston fire of 1838.

Carvalho painted the synagogue of his childhood from memory, both an exterior view and a rendering of the beautiful interior. From his recollection, and from the prints that copied his works, we can understand not only what the building looked like, but something of the great dignity of that house of worship. The Beth Elohim Museum displays Carvalho's painting of the synagogue's interior.

The second synagogue was quickly built on the grounds of the first and was consecrated early in 1841. When a picture of the first building is compared to the current structure, the same wrought iron fence can be seen. It is elegant in its simplicity; only the gate, crowned by scrollwork, is fancifully ornamental and reminiscent of the lost building.

The later synagogue, a beauty in its own right, is often described as one of the finest examples of Greek Revival architecture in the country. A brilliant white building, its front is defended by six enormous fluted Ionic columns, subtly narrowing from base to top. The synagogue has been designated a National Historic Landmark.

The museum is in the administration building behind the Temple. In addition to the Carvalho painting, it holds the original Grant of Arms of the Salvador family. Francis Salvador was the first Jew elected to the colonial legislature, and the first Jew killed during the Revolution. There are displays of items from the Hebrew Benevolent Society, the nation's oldest Jewish charitable organization, and the Hebrew Orphan Society, both of which originated in this congregation. There are various ceremonial objects, photos, portraits of important people, and artifacts that allude to the community's history. A few ancient minute books and other documents survived, but most of the congregation's treasures were carted off to Columbia for safety during the Civil War and were destroyed there by Union troops.

In 1824, a group of 47 congregants of Beth Elohim petitioned the trustees of the synagogue to change the Sephardic Orthodox liturgy. They asked for English translation of the prayers and sermons as well as vocal music. By a vote of just 46 to 40, the changes were approved and led to the congregation's becoming the birthplace of Reform Judaism in the United States. But, as happened so often in such circumstances, dissension divided the congregation and a splinter group went on to build their own Orthodox synagogue. Members of families riven by the split stopped speaking to one another. After the Civil War had left the entire city prostrate, the hostility between the two congregations was forgotten.

Highlight: *In the museum are photographs of and documents relating to what is known as the Coming Street cemetery. Its original name was Beth Haim —House of Living —a name many old Sephardic congregations used to signify their belief in the soul's life after death.*

Fifteen years after the congregation was started, before the synagogue was built and 25 years before the Revolutionary War, this cemetery was established. It remains the oldest Jewish burial ground extant in the South. Unlike Christian cemeteries, which are often right beside a church, Jewish burial grounds are usually at some distance from the synagogue.

Wonderful stories are attached to the cemetery. For instance, David Lopez, though a leading member of the congregation, was not permitted to bury his wife in its cemetery because she had been born a Christian and never formally converted to Judaism. Lopez bought a small piece of land adjacent to the cemetery. There, under a stone canopy, he buried both his wife and their infant son. This narrow plot, once the Lopez plot, is now incorporated into the main Beth Haim.

The Orthodox splinter group that left Beth Elohim in anger established its cemetery right next to the old one, but separated from it by a wall. After the nation's Civil War ended, and with it the hostility between the congregations, the wall was torn down, and the two Jewish cemeteries were united.

TENNESSEE

✒ THE SHAHN MOSAIC ✒

THE TEMPLE
Congregation Ohabai Sholom
5015 Harding Road
Nashville, TN 37205
615-352-7620
Hours: By appointment.

*Have we not all one Father? Hath not one God created us? Why
do we deal treacherously every man against his brother, profaning the
covenant of our fathers?*

These words from the Book of Malachi, in Hebrew, in gold,
float across the top of a mosaic designed by Ben Shahn, *The Call of
the Shofar*. The words are licked by flames but pass over them. A
blue hand, showing both the creative and destructive power of the
Lord, emerges from the flames. Beneath the fire, on the left, is a
menorah; on the right, a man is blowing a shofar, with his head
covered by a prayer shawl. His too large hands hold the long shofar
that is etched with delicate geometric patterns. Below it are five
heads representing the five races.

This mosaic masterpiece, measuring 4 by 14 feet, is seen upon
entering the temple vestibule. Ben Shahn, who died in 1969, was a
leading American Jewish artist. His attitude toward being Jewish was
complicated, as was, and is, that of many artists. Shahn had immigrated from Lithuania at the age of 8. During the 1930s, he was
preoccupied with American politics, the exploitation of the working
classes, and the country's social problems. Concern with human
rights, justice, and religion, recognizable throughout his works, is
apparent as one enters this house of worship. The mosaic occupies a
position of importance and sets a tone that is spiritual and temporal.

The inclusion of works of art was integral to the planning of
the building, which was dedicated in 1955. Jewish holidays are

illustrated in impressive stained-glass windows by A. Raymond Katz. Also by Katz is a brass menorah with a base that resembles a walking figure, a curious and beautiful piece.

The inscription on a bronze menorah by Ludwig Wolpert was taken from Psalm 95, which begins the Sabbath service: "O come let us sing unto the Lord; let us shout for joy to the Rock of our salvation." Proverbs 3:18; "It is a tree of life to them that take hold of it," inspired a bronze sculpture called *The Miracle* by Jacques Lipchitz.

In addition to the original works of art commissioned or purchased for this temple, reproductions of ancient archaeological relics from Israel and photographs of important documents are in display cases.

Highlight: *Works of art also embellish the outside of this building. In the sculpture garden is an arch, The Pomegranate Gate, created by New York artist Oded Halchmy. On the curved exterior facade of the chapel is a formidable, 10-foot-high semiabstract limestone sculpture in which Truth, Justice, and Peace are illustrated by the forms of three rabbis. This powerful work was designed by A. Raymond Katz and executed by Nathaniel Kaz.*

❧ FAMILY = COMMUNITY ❧

JEWISH FEDERATION ARCHIVES
801 Percy Warner Boulevard
Nashville, TN 37205
615-356-7170
Hours: Monday through Friday, 9 to 1, and by appointment.

Among the 26 photographs in an exhibit on The History of the Jews of Nashville, there are many family portraits for, as the Federation's brochure says, in large bold letters, "The History of Your Family is the History of Your Community."

In the beginning—1851, in this community—there were five families and eight single young men in Nashville. By 1983, the number had grown to almost 5,000. In 1853, Nashville got its first rabbi, Alexander Iser, from New York. By 1920, there were six Jewish houses of worship in the city.

Highlight: A 30-minute program, available in videotape and slide/ cassette format, shows how a small group of Southern Jews organized itself to respond to the local, national, and international events that shaped its history. The presentation combines personal narratives with other materials to illustrate the initial influx of German immigrants, the Civil War, the arrival of Eastern European refugees, the Holocaust, and the World Wars.

TEXAS

❧ THAT ADDED SPARKLE ☙

DALLAS JEWISH HISTORICAL SOCIETY
7900 Northaven Road
Dallas, TX 75230
214-739-2737, ext. 261
Hours: Monday, Tuesday, Thursday, 10 to 3; Sunday, 12 to 5.

In this collection are family and institutional papers, photographs, oral histories, and some memorabilia. The Society uses these materials to mount exhibits such as The Great Department Stores: Vanished Names of the Pioneer Jewish Merchants, and a show that must have been a winner, That Added Sparkle: Jews and Jewelry in Dallas.

Both the Historical Society and the Memorial Center (next entry) are housed in the Jewish Community Center of Dallas.

❧ FRAIL WEB ☙

THE DALLAS MEMORIAL CENTER FOR HOLOCAUST STUDIES
7900 Northaven Road
Dallas, TX 75230
214-750-4654
Hours: Sunday through Friday, 10 to 4, all year; Thursday, 10 to 9, September through May.

In October 1977, a group of Holocaust survivors formed an organization that would enable them to relate their experiences and help them to contend with the effect of the Holocaust on their lives. Their impressive effort was realized through this center, in which there are now a library, a memorial, and a museum.

The visit begins in the entry stairwell, where exhibits change. One temporary display was a tapestry illustrating poems about the Holocaust.

At the bottom of the stairs is a boxcar, donated by the National Belgian Railway System; it was once used to transport people to death camps.

The permanent exhibits are chronological and begin with the life of European Jews before World War II. The rise and spread of Nazism, the ghettos, and Hitler's planned extermination of the Jewish people are all explored, as is the liberation. Photographs and memorabilia, such as identification cards, Warsaw ghetto currency, prison uniforms, and films are evidence of the events that are beyond comprehension.

The Memorial Room is entered through cast iron "Gates of Fire" that symbolize the burning of the Torah and of Jewish prayer books. A granite memorial stone is surrounded by twelve marble pillars that stand for the camps in which Dallas survivors were interned. At the head of the memorial stone is a sculpture of a hand reaching out from within a flame. Plaques on the walls bear the names of survivors and of many who died. One wall remains blank in recognition of the lost generations caused by the destruction of the Holocaust.

Highlight: *Words of John dos Passos are used to express the spirit of the Dallas Center: "Our only hope will lie in the frail web of understanding of one person for the pain of another."*

❧ REMBRANDT ❧

KIMBELL ART MUSEUM
3333 Camp Bowie Boulevard
Fort Worth, TX 76107
817-332-8451
Hours: Tuesday to Friday, 10 to 5; Saturday, noon to 8;
Sunday, noon to 5.

The Kimbell is one of the most beautiful, if not the most beautiful, small art museums in the United States. "Their total experience should be warmth, mellowness and even elegance." This was founding director Richard F. Brown's prescription for visitors to the Kimbell when he was creating the museum in 1966. Architect Louis Kahn set new standards for museum design in following Brown's prescription.

One of Brown's major acquisitions as director was Rembrandt's *Portrait of a Young Jew*, dated 1663. How do we know the young man in the picture is a Jew? He wears a black yarmulke, for one thing. Rembrandt lived in the Jewish quarter of Amsterdam, a place known as a relatively safe haven for Jews expelled from Spain during the Spanish Inquisition. Some scholars have even tried out a speculation that Rembrandt himself may have been Jewish because he painted so many pictures of the people who lived in the Jewish quarter.

The background of the painting at the Kimbell is dark, as are the man's clothing and hair. The light shines only on his face, illuminating dark, nearly lashless eyes, a tense forehead and eyebrows, a pallid complexion, a scraggly beard, and soft, moist red lips. Yet, so much expression is in this face that, looking into it, a viewer can see the artist's understanding, compassion, and absorption in the character and emotion of his subject.

By capturing the struggle of one mid-17th-century young Jewish man, Rembrandt has given an insight into the spiritual struggle of all Jews.

◄ OBJECTS OF AFFECTION ►

JUDAICA MUSEUM OF HOUSTON
Congregation Beth Yeshurun
4525 Beechnut Boulevard
Houston, TX 77096-1801
713-666-1881
Hours: By appointment during office hours, Monday through Friday.

In the early 1960s, a small group of enthusiasts began to buy examples of Jewish ceremonial objects for their new synagogue building. They hoped that a Judaica museum would someday be established. Finally, in 1983, the doors to this museum opened, in a wing of the synagogue complex.

There are some paintings and prints in the collection but the concentration here is on Judaica.

A silver-gilt etrog container in this museum follows a popular design—the shape of the lemon-like etrog itself. The etrog is put into a container for protection when being transported to the synagogue for the fall festival of Succoth.

During the eight-day Succoth, meals are eaten under a leafy roof in a specially made hut. It is a pastoral, Thanksgiving-like celebration. At the high point of the synagogue service, the etrog is held in one hand and a lulav, or palm branch, is held in the other.

Another favorite item of Judaica is spice boxes, and the Houston collection has a 19th-century silver filigree spice tower to hold the aromatic herbs—perhaps myrtle, or eucalyptus—that usher out the Sabbath. Spice boxes may range in size from a very small nutmeg grinder to a very large turret. This one, an Austro-Hungarian piece, has a simple design and a pennant at its top. This version is usually about 10 inches high, and was made in large numbers between the middle of the 19th century and World War I.

A collection such as this gives members of a community a chance to see and think about traditions that have often been set aside. Some of the objects are rare and valuable in terms of money, but all of the objects are culturally valuable, for they were used with affection for and appreciation of the tradition they represented.

Highlight: *Marriage belts with elaborate buckles and large links became popular in Germany during the 16th and 17th centuries. The bride and groom each wore one and they were connected during the ceremony. The belt in this museum is from early 17th-century Germany, and is made of silver gilt.*

🍢 ETHICS AND MORALITY 🍢

ROBERT I. KAHN GALLERY
Congregation Emanu-El
1500 Sunset Boulevard
Houston, TX 77005
713-529-5771
Hours: Monday through Friday, 9 to 4; evenings and weekends, by special arrangement.

A visitor can sense the excitement and pride that went into the foundation of this collection and its programs, especially when one speaks with the chairperson of the Art Committee, Joan

Morgenstern. She described the Festival of the Bible in the Arts, held at the Temple in 1960, and its enthusiastic, citywide reception.

The theme was the Bible's influence on the creative minds of artists. The celebration brought together both the visual and the performing arts. The organizers borrowed works of art for the duration and, "When things were back to normal," Morgenstern said, "we realized something wonderful had happened." The Committee wanted that wonderful spirit to continue, and that is when they started their art collection.

The congregation's permanent collection of nearly 300 works includes art by John Singer Sargent, Andy Warhol, Salvador Dali, Jim Dine, Ben Shahn, Leonard Baskin, and others. Artists are both Jewish and non-Jewish, but the subjects of the works had to be of Jewish ethical and moral concern.

Among the holdings is Warhol's series of silk-screened portraits, *Ten Jews of the 20th Century*: Groucho, Chico, and Harpo Marx (in one portrait); Albert Einstein (religion makes strange bedfellows); Franz Kafka; Sarah Bernhardt; Golda Meir; Louis Brandeis; Sigmund Freud; Gertrude Stein; George Gershwin; and Martin Buber.

A fascinating piece is a serigraph, *Ten Commandments* by Paul Levy. Instead of writing the commandments out in script, the artist has designed them as road signs. Inside red circles that are struck through with a red line for the Do Nots, he has the words Polytheism, Idol, God Damn It!, Kill, and so on. The Dos, of which there are just two, are in open green circles with the words Rest and Dad Mom.

Another work that represents the adventurous spirit of this collection is a photograph by John Allerman called *A Matter of Conscience*. It shows a note stuck under a windshield wiper on someone's car. "I think I may have hit your car," the message reads.

The schedule of temporary exhibitions also breaks with convention. During 1989, for example, the Robert I. Kahn Gallery was the only religious institution to host a traveling exhibition called Art and the Law. Thirty-six contemporary artists commented on issues such as homelessness, abuse, the death penalty, and gun control, in imagery that was difficult to imagine being exhibited in a less enlightened or sophisticated community.

VIRGINIA

❦ MEYERS MANSION ❧

MOSES MEYERS HOUSE
323 East Freemason Street
Norfolk, VA
Hours: Tuesday through Saturday: January through March, noon
to 5; April through December, 10 to 5; Sunday, noon to 5.
For further information, contact:
The Chrysler Museum
Olney Road and Mowbray Arch
Norfolk, VA 23510
804-620-1211, ext. 283

Moses Meyers and his partner Samuel Meyers (not a relative) had an export business, with offices in Amsterdam, Holland, and St. Eustatia in the West Indies. Persistent though the partners were, post-Revolutionary War economic difficulties led to bankruptcy— of their finances, not their spirit.

"In Virginia," Moses wrote to Samuel, who was then in Amsterdam, "money is yet to be made." Samuel tried Richmond first, but bad business dealings and a warehouse fire convinced him to move on to Norfolk. Like Richmond, Norfolk had been devastated by fire during the war, but on the other side of their disaster was a promise of recovery.

In March 1787, Moses married a young widow, Eliza, and that summer they sailed to Norfolk on a schooner named *Sincerity*. They were among the first Jews to settle in Norfolk, and, without a congregation, they practiced their religion privately, at home. Eliza wore a small portrait of her husband, a brooch painted on an oval of ivory and framed in gold, blue enamel, and seed pearls. A lock of his hair is tucked into the back of the case. He looks young despite his grey wig, and seems to have a quizzical look, as though unsure whether to smile or frown.

In August, Moses and Samuel announced the debut of their new venture and its wares: "naval stores, corn, bees-wax, deer skins, tobacco and lumber of all sorts in abundance, very good and cheap."

The Dismal Swamp Canal opened to connect the inland waterways of North Carolina with Chesapeake Bay, and the city of Norfolk prospered. The fortunes and the family of Eliza and Moses grew. He would soon own two schooners, one of which he named after his wife. They had 12 children, but only 9 survived infancy. In 1789, Samuel Meyers left the partnership.

In 1792, the Meyers built themselves a fine brick house in Norfolk, so situated that they could stand out on the side porch and watch the port activity, their own ships in particular. By the outbreak of the War of 1812, Moses was doing business in every seaport on both sides of the North Atlantic, and his eldest son, John, was in his twenties and a partner in Moses Meyer & Son. (The next son, Samuel, is thought to have been the first Jew to matriculate at the College of William and Mary at Williamsburg. Samuel became a lawyer and married Louisa Marx of Richmond; see page 183.)

The Meyers' house still stands today, a lovely mansion in the Federal style, two stories high, with an elegant fanlight under the eaves. The neighborhood now has parking lots and office buildings all around, but most of the furnishings inside the house belonged to the original owners. This is a rare instance where a house stayed in one family for five generations.

Moses and Eliza sat for their portraits, which were painted by no less a celebrity than Gilbert Stuart. Moses was 54, wigless but somewhat closer to a smile than in the tiny portrait. Eliza was 42 and about to have her twelfth child. She looks youthful, with ruddy red cheeks—a Gilbert Stuart conceit, if not her own. She wears a low-cut, white, Empire style gown and, curiously, the shape of her face and outline of her features seem almost to duplicate those of Moses. Did they grow to resemble one another? Or is this how Stuart saw them?

The Moses Meyers house is a beautiful restoration that offers an exceptional opportunity to see original furnishings. Entering the raised front portico, one discovers an unusual architectural feature: the expansive front hall opens to the right and to the left, rather than following the conventional scheme of proceeding straight ahead. The ceiling is embellished with molding that has a snowflakelike pattern, and there is a very tall and handsome case clock.

Exterior of Moses Meyers House, Norfolk, Virginia. Courtesy of The Chrysler Museum.

One does not see any real evidence of the Meyers' Judaism. There is some Judaica—a menorah, for example—but it is of more recent vintage, bought for the house after it became a museum. A moment of eclipse came in 1877, when Meyer Meyers's widow, Judith, converted to Christianity.

Meyer was Eliza and Moses's fifth child. Judith Marx Meyers was a sister of Louisa Marx of Richmond, who married Meyer's brother Samuel. Judith waited until after the death of her father, her husband, and her father-in-law, but then she converted. Her reasons are uncertain. She was very active in society and perhaps wished to erase those differences which appeared to set her apart from the largely Christian group with whom she associated.

In 1931, the Colonial House Corporation bought the Meyers property and its furnishings, in order to preserve the house as an historic landmark. In 1951, the City of Norfolk received the house, by deed, from the Corporation. The house is now administered by the Chrysler Museum.

Highlight: *In the early 1960s, Floyd Painter, an archaeologist working for the Norfolk Museum, undertook to dig in the well that was discovered beneath the porch and steps leading to the Meyers' back yard. He reported his findings in 1962: a foot-by-foot descent through "wood ashes with broken glass, bones of animal, fish and fowl from a well varied menu, chinaware, bottles and broken crockery, all easily identified as late nineteenth century." His report is one of the most hilarious archaeological documents in print. "At two-and-one-half feet we began striking oyster shells and broken bricks . . . quantities of late nineteenth century material which included glass chimneys from kerosene lamps, clay marbles, a small lead figure of a man on a bicycle plus the aforementioned bric-a-brac of the top stratum. Hopes still high, well getting deeper."*

The litany goes on, and on, and on. With oyster shells in overwhelming abundance, the going was fetid and malodorous. "The material from the thirteen foot level was contemporary with that at the top; the well had been filled in a very short time. . . . Our spirits were now lower than the water table, we climbed out and the water rose behind us." The list of objects is extremely uninteresting, from a historical or archaeological point of view. "I suggested that the old well be restored . . . but that was expensive. Now the well has been refilled with rubble and earth and a concrete walk laid over it, a dummy or imitation well has been built in the back yard to enhance the setting of the garden and grounds. So much for restoration."

Much merriment resulted from the archaeologist's widely reported discovery of the Moses Meyers spittoon. "All this would be detrimental to my dignity if I had any," he wrote. But, what he had he'd lost five years earlier when he unearthed the personal chamber pot of Madame Sarah Thorogood and, he wrote, "What greater rewards could an archaeologist hope to attain?"

⫷ ALL IN THE FAMILY ⫸

CONGREGATION BETH AHABAH MUSEUM AND
ARCHIVES TRUST
1109 West Franklin Street
Richmond, VA 23220
804-353-2668
Hours: Monday, 10 to 3; Tuesday and Wednesday, 10 to 4;
Thursday, 10 to 2.

"On the north side of the James River is lately laid off a town with streets sixty-five feet wide, in a pleasant and healthy situation and well supplied with springs of good water." So advertised William Byrd II, in 1737, in his effort to establish Richmond, Virginia, as a center of commerce. Still, fewer than a thousand people had settled there when Isaiah Isaacs arrived in 1769. He may have doubted the wisdom of his move two years later, when the river sent a 40-foot-high wall of water roaring through the wide streets, sweeping away the ships, houses, warehouses, and stores in its path.

Isaacs was the first Jew who settled in Richmond, as far as anyone knows. Did he attend the gathering at St. John's Church in March 1775, and hear Patrick Henry issue his impassioned cry for liberty or death? Isaacs probably kept a low profile, because colonial Virginia sternly and exclusively professed Anglicanism (the only legal form of worship). Jews weren't outlawed, but they weren't encouraged either. More likely, they considered themselves forewarned by the example of some Baptist ministers who were beaten and sent to jail in 1774 for preaching their version of the word of God.

The situation improved after the Revolution and the passage of Thomas Jefferson's Bill for Establishing Religious Freedom—a Virginia statute that was signed into law on January 19, 1786. Isaacs and his associate, Jacob I. Cohen, owned what may have been the first hotel in town, Bird in the Hand Inn and Tavern, known around town as the "Jews' Store." In December 1786, Isaacs and Cohen advertised in the newspaper a boarding house next door to the inn. Their fortunes were growing. They held slaves, real estate, and lead mines, and at one point hired Daniel Boone to survey their land in Kentucky (see page 106).

Richmond's attraction increased. By 1789, there were between 20 and 30 Jewish families in town and a synagogue was formed, Beth Shalome (House of Peace), one of the first six synagogues in the country. The others were in Newport, New York, Charleston (then Charles Town), Savannah, and Philadelphia.

The Jewish community was a small world with lovely synergies of familial connection. An early Richmond worthy, for example, Joseph Marx, married Richea Meyers, daughter of the renowned New York silversmith Meyer Meyers. Marx also had many business dealings with Moses Meyers, whose home in Norfolk is now a museum. Two of his daughters married sons of Moses Meyers. (See the previous entry.)

Richmond's prosperity was interrupted from time to time, but just before the Civil War it was vigorous: there were ironworks and cotton mills, and the export business in flour and tobacco was lively. Ships that sailed for South America with Virginia flour returned with coffee beans. As Virginians and slaveholders, Southern Jews fought for the South. Richmond was the capital of the Confederate States of America, and the terrible wages of the war were redoubled when retreating Confederate troops set the city ablaze so that Union soldiers would not benefit from what they left behind.

Jewish life of early Richmond is told in this museum and archives through ephemera, artifacts, and ceremonial objects. Examples include the advertisement that appeared in the *Virginia Gazette* in 1786, announcing Cohen and Isaacs' Bird in the Hand Inn and Tavern; 18th-century scales brought from Germany, used by a local merchant for weighing gold; and one of Meyer Meyers' works in silver—a small, simple, and exquisite oval snuff box with a hidden clasp and little ball feet. There are also two 19th-century portraits of

Maximilian and Miriam Angle Michelbacher. He was the first rabbi of Beth Ahabah (House of Love), with which Beth Shalome eventually merged.

One object of unusual significance is a stone measuring some three by four by two feet and weighing about 500 pounds; a hydraulic lift was required to hoist it onto its pedestal. This is the cornerstone of a synagogue near Hanover, Germany, which was burned during Kristallnacht, November 9 and 10, 1938. The cornerstone was rescued and brought to America by a member of the congregation who had been bar mitzvahed in the vanished synagogue. It is among the collection's most cherished pieces.

Highlight: *The museum is located in a brownstone house next door to the synagogue. If you call ahead, you will probably be able to make arrangements to visit the magnificent sanctuary, which has a signed Tiffany window that looks like the image of a volcano. It is meant to represent Mount Sinai erupting at the very moment Moses received the Ten Commandments.*

WISCONSIN

GIFTS

JOSEPH BARON MUSEUM
Congregation Emanuel B'ne Jeshurun
2419 East Kenwood Boulevard
Milwaukee, WI 53211
414-964-4100
Hours: Whenever the synagogue is open; call before visiting.

The major part of this collection is on display in the main lobby of the synagogue.

Annette Hirsh, a silversmith who specializes in Judaica objects, has been the moving spirit of the museum for the past 20 years. The collection was launched in 1936 with congregants' gifts. They were people mainly of German heritage and they donated pieces that they had brought with them to this country. The museum was reorganized in 1951 by the rabbi whose name it now carries.

The collection contains about 350 objects, paintings, prints, and sculpture. Each year, there are six small exhibits on Jewish subjects, both historic and contemporary.

Highlight: *Etrog boxes come in various shapes, sizes, and materials. Many are in the form of the oval citrus fruit they are made to hold, but numerous others are box-shaped and as gorgeous as if they were to hold the finest jewels. A box in this collection is in the latter category. Made in Jerusalem during the early 20th century, it is brass inlaid with copper and silver. Stylized figures represent the rabbi and congregants praying in the synagogue; symbolic objects, from the menorah and eternal light to the bimah (the platform and desk where the Torah is read), are all expressively engraved.*

Early 20th-century brass etrog box from Jerusalem. Courtesy of Joseph Baron Museum, Congregation Emanuel B'ne Jeshurun.

WEST

ARIZONA

❧ FRONTIER LIFE ❧

ARIZONA JEWISH HISTORICAL SOCIETY
Greater Phoenix Chapter
4143 North 12th Street, Suite 100-D
Phoenix, AZ 85014
602-241-7870
Hours: By appointment.

Hollywood depictions of the Old West notwithstanding, cities had begun to become major commercial centers, and a full and prosperous life could be lived far from a home on the range or cavalry sorties against "hostiles." Arizona, even then, was appealing for its climate and beauty and its potential for future growth and security. A whole new West was beginning to emerge, and wise investors and entrepreneurs gave their best efforts to get in on the ground floor. The Goldwater family (see page 106) may be the most famous name surviving from that era, but they were only one of many astute and successful Jewish families who did not let a chance for prosperity pass them by. There had to be a recognizable number of Jewish voters in Phoenix by the 1880s, because the city elected a Jewish mayor.

That Jews participated in all facets of Western frontier life is graphically illustrated by this collection. The library is devoted to both Arizona's history and that of the state's Jewish community.

187

Library resources continue to grow, as does the small collection of artifacts. The walls of the Society's large office are covered with photographs of Arizona's Jewish pioneers, and early buildings and street scenes.

Available for study is a small exhibit of outstanding Jewish women from pioneer days to the present.

Highlight: *In 1989, the Society mounted a traveling exhibition with about 100 photographs on the subject of Arizona's Jewish settlement, from the major cities of Prescott, Phoenix, and Tucson to hamlets with names like Globe, Holbrook, Benson, and Clifton. One dazzling photo was of the Phoenix Carnival Queen of 1899 and her attendants. Lillie Solomon, daughter of I. E. Solomon, who founded a major bank, was the second from the left; Hazel Goldberg, who had two long curls resting on her shoulders and a pouty face, was seated at the queen's right hand, the spot usually given to a beauty queen's runner-up.*

❧ TUNISIAN LEGACY ❧

PLOTKIN JUDAICA MUSEUM OF GREATER PHOENIX
Temple Beth Israel
3310 North 10th Avenue
Phoenix, AZ 85013
602-264-4428
Hours: Tuesday, Wednesday, and Thursday, 10 to 3 (docent tours, 10 to 2); Friday evening, after services; Sunday, 12 to 3. Three weeks' notice is required for private tours for groups of ten or more.

Steven Orlikoff, a young man with blond, curly hair, was a student of International Relations at the University of Southern California. In 1971, he went off to live, work, and study in Tunis for a year. He found a Jewish community there that natives believe originated with the First Temple (built by Solomon in Jerusalem and destroyed in 586 B.C.E.).

Jews had prospered in Tunisia; their communities flourished during the Roman Empire and continued until the 11th and 12th centuries, when Arab persecutions began. At the turn of the 20th century, the Jews of Tunisia, under the French protectorate, had unprecedented freedom and the population reached 200,000. With the creation of the Moslem Republic in 1956, decline began again, and when Orlikoff was there in 1971, the population was down to about 8,000 and still decreasing. Fewer than half of that number remain there today; most are elderly people.

Among the friends Orlikoff made in Tunis was a couple who told him about their small family synagogue that had been founded around 1870. It closed in 1970, was soon vandalized, and was suffering from neglect. Orlikoff's family were longtime members of Beth Israel in Phoenix and the temple's museum was offered the remaining artifacts from the Tunisian synagogue. These were moved, piece by piece, over a period of four years.

Orlikoff's Tunisian friends must be credited for one of the most unusual Jewish museum displays in this country. An exhibit called Tunisian Legacy is a recreated, composite neighborhood synagogue. In addition to the artifacts from the abandoned Tunisian synagogue, such as a traditional Sephardic Torah case (a tik—a single, rigid holder rather than the more familiar scroll wound around two poles and covered with a fabric mantle), there are a number of other Middle Eastern artifacts.

The design for the Tunisian Legacy gallery is based on a synagogue on the Island of Djerba, just off the Tunisian coast. This community, which dates back to 586 B.C.E., according to legend, may have been the very first North African settlement. Its island location kept it somewhat isolated and made it a more persuasive example of ancient village life. Of its 80,000 inhabitants today, only 1,000 are Jewish. It is said that the settlers brought with them a door from Solomon's Temple, around which they built their first synagogue, called La Ghirba. La Ghirba is the model for the arches and the ark of the Phoenix exhibit. The colorful tiles are set in elaborate Islamic designs, and the entire effect is stunning visually and intriguing because it has transplanted the religious aura of a distant time and place.

The museum is the project of Sylvia Plotkin, whose husband has been rabbi at Temple Beth Israel since the 1950s. She went back to school, at the age of 41, to pursue museum studies for this endeavor. Founded in 1967, the museum was named after the Plotkins, to honor the rabbi's 25th anniversary of service at the temple.

Today, there are twenty-five docents who have signed up for a two-year course in which they learn about Jewish history through the artifacts. Their immersion in museum work amplifies their education.

In the main gallery of the Museum, the exhibit is based on the theme of Holiness, and Jewish life over time and in many countries is explored. An active program of traveling exhibits, as well as an ongoing series of films, lectures, symposia, and videos, are conducted under the Museum's sponsorship.

Highlight: *The Tunisian exhibit is the outstanding distinction at this museum, but there is a good deal more to see. Among the contemporary works are two sculptures by American women, both done during the 1980s, that merit particular attention. One is a very still bronze,* Waiting for the Tenth Man, *in which a group of nine robed men, books in hand, are standing together, but each man is somehow solitary.*

Another bronze, Out of the Ashes, *is entirely different. A pyramidlike pile of bodies, distraught and writhing, is reaching up to the peak of the pyramid where the Magen David — the Star of David — is seen on the flag of Israel.*

CALIFORNIA

✎ PAINT, MOP, POLISH, AND PURPOSE ✐

JUDAH L. MAGNES MUSEUM
2911 Russell Street
Berkeley, CA 94705
415-849-2710
Hours: Sunday through Thursday, 10 to 4.

In the earliest days of this museum, the exhibition schedule and process were informal, to say the least. The curator put five to ten objects in his car and delivered them to various locations in the San Francisco Bay area. Yet, these mini-exhibits served their purpose. They aroused the curiosity of the public and drew attention to the Jewish presence not only in California but throughout the West.

The first home of the collection was in one room of Oakland's Jewish Community Center. In the early 1960s, it moved to larger quarters, over the Parkway Theater. The theater's owner, Jesse Levin, was a friend who donated the space, rent-free.

In 1966, a small group of generous supporters bought a large brick building known as the Burke Mansion. Volunteers painted and mopped, and polished the glass display cases that had been donated by local merchants. Not only did local people contribute time and devotion, helping to search out items of importance throughout the world, but the reputation of the Magnes and of the objects it had collected began to circulate throughout the country. This is a story of vision and growth in which the sense of purpose and the determination of a few people brought about the evolution of a major institution.

Foremost among these people is Seymour Fromer, founder and director of the museum. To him, the local community seemed to have very little Jewish identity or sense of history. One day, while on a foraging expedition in a second-hand book store, Fromer came across an 1893 issue of the Oakland High School magazine. In it he

Lavater and Lessing Visit Moses Mendelssohn by Mortiz Daniel Oppenheim.
Courtesy of Judah L. Magnes Museum, Berkeley, California.

Esther by Ephraim Moses Lilien, 1923. Courtesy of Judah L. Magnes Museum, Berkeley, California.

Maurice Sendak, illustration for *Zlateh the Goat and Other Stories* by Isaac Bashevis Singer, 1966. Courtesy of Judah L. Magnes Museum, Berkeley, California.

The "Song of Songs" rug of the Bezalel School (Jerusalem, ca. 1920) derives its name from the biblical quotations in Hebrew on the ground. Courtesy of Judah L. Magnes Museum, Berkeley, California.

195

discovered a picture of Judah L. Magnes, who graduated in 1893. While researching the life of Judah Magnes, Seymour Fromer found the idea he needed to make a presentation of the Jewish presence in the West begin to coalesce.

Judah Magnes was an interesting man. Born in San Francisco in 1877, he grew up in Oakland and was the first native Californian to be ordained a rabbi—and the first rabbi ordained west of the Mississippi. His career took him far and wide: he was a co-founder of the Hebrew University of Jerusalem, Hadassah, and the American Civil Liberties Union, and he played a part in establishing the Joint Distribution Committee which provided relief to European Jews during and after World War I.

But Magnes was also a controversial figure. As a pacifist, he opposed American entry into World War I—a very unpopular position to take. He believed that Israel should be a binational state in which Arabs and Jews lived together equally. Magnes was one of the founders of Berit Shalom (The Peace Association). The organization, established in 1925 in Jerusalem and composed of Jewish intellectuals, sought to foster friendly relations between Arab and Jews.

When the Magnes Museum celebrated its 25th anniversary in 1987, curators reviewed their treasures and chose 25 pieces to highlight their collection. Among them is a large oil painting, *Jews Crying Near the Wall of Solomon*. The artist was a Russian, Vassili Vereshchagin (1842–1904). He commented, "This part of the wall which surrounded the Temple is called The Wailing Place because the Jews for a long time past have been in the habit of coming hither to bewail their past greatness and present dispersion. Seldom can anything more touching be seen." And seldom is the Wailing Wall so powerfully shown. The massive stones occupy nearly three-quarters of the canvas and a host of small human figures are in the lowest quarter. They are intense in postures of both prayer and conversation.

Another work of strong emotional content is a painting by Lazar Krestin, a Lithuanian-born Jew who studied in Vienna and Munich. Called *The Birth of Jewish Resistance*, it was painted in the aftermath of the bloody pogrom of Kishinev, Bessarabia, during Easter of 1903. The work shows a group of workers who have taken up arms in self-defense. The expressions on their faces are resigned rather than angry; they are stunned but determined to protect themselves. The pogrom had left many Jews dead and injured, and thousands of homes and businesses were destroyed. It generated self-defense societies such as the one represented here.

Among the fascinating stories of the Jewish diaspora is that of the settlers in Cochin, a city and former state in Southwest India. The Cochin Jews were protected by the rajahs during the 16th and 17th centuries—the period of Spanish and Portugese persecution in Europe. The Dutch, who dominated India from 1663 to 1795, gave the Jews of Cochin cultural autonomy and religious freedom.

At the Magnes is an oil-burning bronze lamp from Cochin. Its inscription in Hebrew notes that it was given to the synagogue of Parur in 1670. In 1685, a delegation of four Jews from Amsterdam went to Cochin and received an emotional, affectionate reception. They also wrote about this lamp: "Unlike the brass oil lamps used in Hindu Temples and houses, this lamp is unique. . . . designed for Jews especially for the Day of Atonement Service, as the oil in the lamp will be sufficient for lighting for more than twenty-four hours." Just 18 inches high, this object becomes monumental in the light of its history.

The Magnes has had a lively exhibition schedule over its years of operation. Many of the exhibits have originated here, others have come on loan. Contemporary Jewish artists have been shown, and themes have ranged from the experience of Kurdish Jews in Israel, the role of magic in Jewish tradition, and the customs and costumes of Jews in Turkey to the irresistible *The Yiddische Gauchos*, an exhibit and video documentary tracing the creation of late 19th-century agricultural colonies on the Argentine pampas by Eastern European Jewish settlers.

Highlight: *As part of its regional commitment, the Magnes supports a Western Jewish History Center, which contains archival materials on the Jews of the 13 Western American states. These materials include oral histories, newspapers, periodicals, books, and historic documents. The hours for the Center (in the same building as the museum) are Monday through Thursday, noon to 4. For more information about the Center, call 415-842-2710.*

❧ ONE OF THE BIG FOUR ❧

HEBREW UNION COLLEGE SKIRBALL MUSEUM
32nd and Hoover Streets
Los Angeles, CA
213-749-3424
Hours: Tuesday through Friday, 11 to 4; Sunday, 10 to 5.

Midway between West Los Angeles and the San Fernando Valley, in the Sepulveda Pass of the Santa Monica Mountains and not far from the new J. Paul Getty Center, the Hebrew Union College Skirball Cultural Center is scheduled to open in 1993. It will be an exciting complex on a gorgeous site and has been designed by Moshe Safdie, a Canadian and one of the world's major architects.

The Jewish population of Los Angeles (600,000) is the second largest in the United States, after New York City. The museum that will be included in the Cultural Center will vie with New York's Jewish Museum in importance. Paradoxically, considering the relative ages of the two cities, the Los Angeles collection is older: it was 100 years old in 1976. That needs some explanation.

The collection started at the main Hebrew Union College campus in Cincinnati. It was relocated in 1972 to California, where the potential audience is larger. With 18,000 objects, this is one of the four major Judaica collections in the world. The others are at the Israel Museum, the State Jewish Museum in Prague, and the New York Jewish Museum. Holdings at Skirball include 1,200 archaeological artifacts, 6,000 ceremonial objects and ethnographic materials, 4,000 prints, drawings, and photographs, 1,000 ancient and modern coins and medals, and 300 paintings and sculptures.

The catalog entry for one of the ceremonial artifacts reads: Torah Binder, USA, 1889. The fabric is linen, and along the edges is the plain running stitch all girls used to learn in school. The lettering in both Hebrew and English, states that Gilbert Sanders was born on July 8, 1889. Decorations include a Star of David, a bird, a green wreath, and an American flag. This Torah binder, as was the tradition, is a wimple—it was made from the linen of a male baby's swaddling cloth.

Use of wimples began in Germany during the 16th century. They were usually painted or embroidered with the child's name and date of birth (and often his zodiacal sign). This particular binder was part of an effort to introduce the wimple tradition into Jewish life in the United States. The effort was not successful.

Gilbert Sanders's life was exemplary. He became a lawyer and president of the congregation of his Trinidad, Colorado, synagogue. Trinidad was a late 19th-century coal mining center and had one of the earliest Jewish communities in Colorado. Sanders was awarded an honorary degree by Hebrew Union College, to which he donated his binder. Sanders's wife was president of the Trinidad congregation during the 1950s, probably the first woman in the United States to hold such a position. Moreover, she officiated as acting rabbi for that small Rocky Mountain Jewish community.

The collection of Jewish ceremonial and domestic textiles at this museum is one of the finest in the world. It was largely acquired in 1926; in 1984, the museum began the major endeavor of surveying, preserving, storing, and conserving. A very impressive piece is a 17th-century Torah curtain from Czechoslovakia. The splendor of many of these objects illustrates the Jewish practice of worshipping God in the most beautiful way possible, which was a biblical command. To fulfill that command, people often donated their best or, as in the case of wimples, their most significant finery.

The Skirball's archaeological collection was gathered mainly by Nelson Glueck, a pioneering biblical archaeologist who also served as president of Hebrew Union College. Glueck located King Solomon's mines and foundry at Ezion-Geber, in 1940. Then, in 1965, Glueck reappraised and rejected his own find. The idea of using the bible as a sort of treasure-hunting map is fascinating, but controversy inevitably springs up and the practice comes under attack. The very science of archaeology can then become controversial.

There is drama enough in simply contemplating a Palestinian jug from thousands of years ago. One cannot help but wonder who incised the simple border design just below its neck, who poured from it, and what it held. This, and the other jugs, pitchers, bottles, and bowls are so finely shaped and balanced that they rival the best pottery made today.

Leaping forward in time, a pair of Torah ark lions acquired by the Skirball in 1990 were carved by Marcus Charles Illions, an artist who immigrated to this country from Vilna in 1888. Illions's greatest renown is derived from his carvings of prancing carousel steeds, especially those in the carousel at Brooklyn's Coney Island amusement park. This museum has one of the three American synagogue carvings attributed to him.

Illions's lions are distinctive. Their manes are wavy and full—bouffant, even—and their mouths are wide open. Their expressions are funny rather than fierce. The Skirball pair actually seem to be laughing. (A pair owned by the Jewish Museum in New York (page 66) are more serious but no less silly. Both pairs are dated 1910.)

There is great diversity in the Skirball collection—objects from earliest to most recent times, countries as widespread as the Jewish diaspora, all media, subject matter, and use. The variety is unified only by the fact that each reflects some aspect of Jewish life.

Skirball launched a distinctive collecting project in 1985. The Illions lions fit nicely into this project, which has been named Project Americana.

Highlights: *These are among the artifacts in Project Americana:*

- *A cast brass Hanukkah lamp whose nine branches are topped with reproductions of the Statue of Liberty; an American eagle rises from the central post.*

- *A costume design by Arthur Szyk for a female character in the 1940 Yiddish Art Theater's American production of* Esther. *She is dressed as a Polish servant girl with a striped skirt and bolero, and she has an embroidered purse hanging from her belt.*

- *A can of Rokeach scouring powder "For Cleaning and Polishing" made in Brooklyn, New York, in 1912. The label is red, white, and blue.*

- *A thermometer from Kahn's Department store in Mikado, Michigan.*

- *A butter crock from Mrs. Kaplan's Store in Missouri Valley, Iowa.*

שפייז וועט געווינען דיא קריעג !

איהר קומט אהער צו געפינען פרייהייט.

יעצט מוזט איהר העלפען זיא צו בעשיצען.

מיר מוזען דיא עלליים פערזארגען מיט ווייץ.

לאזט קיין זאך ניט גיין אין ניוועץ

יונייטעד סטייטס שפייז פערוואלטונג.

Immigration poster with Yiddish inscription, published by the U.S. Department of Agriculture during World War I. Courtesy of Hebrew Union College
Skirball Museum; Lelo Carter, photographer.

Torah binder, Germany, 1731, linen embroidered with silk threads. Courtesy of Hebrew Union College Skirball Museum; Lelo Carter, photographer.

Tik Torah case, China, Hunan Province, 17th century; wood gilt lacquered in red bronze. Courtesy of Hebrew Union College Skirball Museum; John Reed Forsman, photographer.

Hanukkah lamp, Germany, 1814, silver gilt. Courtesy of Hebrew Union College Skirball Museum, John Reed Forsman, photographer.

◄ SUR-RATIONAL ◄

PLATT ART GALLERY AND SMALLEY FAMILY SCULPTURE GARDEN
University of Judaism
15600 Mulholland Drive
Los Angeles, CA 90077
213-879-4144/213-476-9777
Hours: Call for details.

Things are just getting started, as far as the collection of art and sculpture on this campus is concerned. The school, which is affiliated with the Jewish Theological Seminary of America, was founded in 1947; the new campus was built in 1985.

The sculpture collection started in 1965 with a 9-foot-tall elliptical bronze piece by Aldo Casanova, called *Juncture*. The artist wrote, "My sculpture attempts to convey the immutable presence of the life force which some call God."

There is recent work by Jenny Holzer, whose single-line phrases are usually jarring and always loaded. This one is a marble bench in a series called *Truism*. Another piece is by Keith Haring, who began as an artist in New York's subway system. His odd figures became familiar to the public before he died in 1989.

The gallery has been devoted mainly to showing temporary exhibitions. A show hosted in spring of 1991 was Sur-Rational Paintings of Fritz Hirschberger. Sur-rational (beyond the reasonable) is a term invented by the artist after he read the diary of a Nazi doctor at Auschwitz.

Hirschberger's father was killed in a concentration camp. The artist, born in 1920 to Polish parents living in Germany, was deported to Poland. He worked as a cotton picker, blacksmith, and camel driver, and joined the Free Polish Army in which he fought against Rommel's forces in North Africa. He was arrested by the Soviets for his Zionist affiliations and sentenced to a labor camp. In 1984, Hirschberger moved to San Francisco.

Hirschberger's sur-rational paintings are strange, in part because of the flat, masklike faces of his people, who seem to fall somewhere between Modigliani and medieval figures. Some of their oddness originates in the colors he uses—fuchsia, purple, and pinks, for example, which are inappropriate for his death camp subjects.

At the close of the exhibit, the university took on the Hirschberger works for its permanent collection.

Highlight: *In a work called* Indifference, *Hirschberger has painted a woman holding a baby, accompanied by three children. They are walking inside the barbed-wire fence of a concentration camp. The ground is dark purple-blue, shades darker than the clothes of the people, who are all seen in profile and wear hoods. Their faces are invisible, except for the baby whose round, startling white face is dotted with features and stares at the viewer.*

The background of this upsetting work is an almost electric fuchsia. A quotation, attributed to E. Yashinski, is written against the background. It reads:

Fear not your enemies for they can only kill you.
Fear not your friends for they can only betray you.
Fear only the indifferent who permit the killers and betrayers
    to walk safely on earth.

❧ STYLE: LEVANTINE ❧

THE ELIZABETH S. FINE MUSEUM OF CONGREGATION EMANU-EL
The Congregation Emanu-El
Arguello Boulevard and Lake Street
San Francisco, CA 94118
415-751-2535
Hours: By appointment.

This temple looks like an extravagant Moorish mosque with a touch of California Mission style. One of the most remarkable synagogues in the country, Temple Emanu-El has an L-shaped plan, and the architectural style, a fusion of Mediterranean and Byzantine, is called Levantine. It is surmounted by a great, red-tiled dome that rises 150 feet above street level. A monumental archway opens into a courtyard with a fountain, surrounded by arcades of columns and porches with vaulted ceilings.

The museum usually exhibits the work of young Jewish artists working in the Bay area. Once or twice a year there is an "archives exhibit": Bible prints, Torah breastplates, and other Judaica. Among the museum's most exceptional works of art is a silver Torah breastplate made in Eastern Europe during the 19th century. It is an elaborate work with traditional symbolic images: a Decalogue in the center is flanked by pillars that are topped by heraldic lions holding a crown. The entire surface is worked with flowers and leafy and vinelike decoration.

Highlight: *The extraordinary bronze ark stands beneath a marble canopy. It was built in London by two California artists. Decorative enamel panels name and illustrate the twelve tribes of Israel. It resembles a jewel box, perhaps to express the preciousness of its contents. Two round handles for carrying the Ark are set into magnificent lion heads.*

❧ BLUE JEANS ☙

LEVI STRAUSS & CO. MUSEUM
250 Valencia Street
Mailing address: Levi Strauss & Co.
Levi's Plaza
P. O. Box 7215
San Francisco, CA 94120
415-565-9160
Hours: Wednesday, tours are given twice; they must be booked in advance.

In January 1848, a strike was made along the Sacramento River on land owned by John August Sutter, a Swiss immigrant.

Gold! All over the country, all over the world, farmers dropped their hoes, sailors jumped ship, shopkeepers closed shop; they all headed west in the California Gold Rush. The announcement brought adventurers to California as if the gold were magnetically charged and the treasure hunters were metal filings.

Among the earliest fortune seekers was Levi Strauss, an immigrant from Bavaria. He was not yet 20 when his brothers outfitted him and sent him to peddle his wares around the mining camps. Before the Gold Rush began, the population of California had been 15,000; by 1852, it was 250,000. Levi Strauss saw clearly and quickly that one thing miners needed was durable clothes.

Levi Strauss, ca. 1890. Courtesy of the Levi Strauss & Co. Archives.

The Levi Strauss & Co. Factory and Museum. Courtesy of the Levi Strauss & Co. Archives.

Strauss had some heavy tent material in his stock and he used it to make his first overalls ("Two Horse Brand Overalls Are Made For Men of Every Trade," according to a 1915 advertisement). His manufacturing business was burgeoning by the 1870s, when the first Levi Strauss factory was built.

The first factory was destroyed during the earthquake and fire of 1906, but there is a museum in the company's oldest surviving factory (built in 1906), a three-story, clapboard building that looks a lot more like an old Western hotel than a factory. Structural posts hold up a railed balcony on the second floor.

Not a lot is known about this German Jewish entrepreneur, because so much documentation was lost when his earliest factory was destroyed. The museum has a photograph of him, a copy of his obituary, and a brief biography. There is also a pair of the earliest pants made by the company, and their evolution to the jeans we know today is described. Other items include vintage machinery, a history of the company as told through its manufacture of other garments, and a history of Levi's long-standing association with the West.

HAWAII

❧ ALOHA, SHALOM ❧

BERNARD H. LEVINSON HAWAIIAN JEWISH ARCHIVES
Temple Emanu-El
2550 Pali Highway
Honolulu, HI 96817
808-595-7521
Hours: Monday through Friday, 9 to 4; call for Sunday hours.

"We have a small collection of ceremonial objects, the majority of which are currently in storage," writes my Honolulu correspondent, Evelyn Trapido. "In addition there are oil lamps, jugs, and spears, mostly reproductions of artifacts from Biblical times. Until we obtain adequate display space, these artifacts may be viewed only by appointment."

The photo collection is the outstanding part of the archive collection. Many of the photographs were prepared for an exhibition called The Wandering Jews: Places of Jewish Worship in Hawaii. To the surprise of many viewers, these showed 30 or more buildings that dated back to the turn of the century.

Highlight: *This is an evolving collection to keep in mind should you visit Hawaii. On permanent exhibit in the temple's social hall are photographs that depict Jewish life in Hawaii from World War II through the 1950s.*

CANADA

QUEBEC

❧ JEWISH LIFE THAT WAS ❧

THE MONTREAL HOLOCAUST MEMORIAL CENTRE
Edifice Cummings
5151, Chemin de la Côte Ste. Catherine
Montreal, Quebec H3W 1M6
514-345-2605
Hours: Sunday through Thursday, 10 to 4. Office: Monday
through Friday, 9 to 5.

The objects in this collection came from Jewish communities in Europe both before and after the Nazi era. Among the memorabilia are:

- A small heart made of paper and cloth, a birthday gift to someone interned in Auschwitz in December 1944.
- A hand-embroidered matzo cover with felt appliqué, which was handed down from mother to daughter for several generations. It survived deportation and internment in Bershad, Transnistria, an area in the Ukraine where 300,000 Jews lived before the Nazi occupation. Two-thirds of the Jewish inhabitants fled, but Transnistria became the destination for 185,000 deported Romanian Jews. More than 200,000 Jews perished there.

- A book, handwritten on parchment, that was a gift to one of the leaders of the Lodz ghetto.

Highlight: Splendor and Destruction: Jewish Life that Was, 1919 to 1945, is a new permanent exhibition that will contain over 20 display cases of art, ceremonial objects, artifacts, and documents. Over two hundred items will be on display.

אֲכִילַת
מַצָּה

Matzo cover, velvet, felt appliqué and embroidery. Czernovitz, Bukovina,
mid-19th century. Survived deportation and internment in Bershad,
Transnistria, 1941–1944. Courtesy of Montreal Holocaust Memorial
Centre.

ONTARIO

❧ REMEMBER ❧

HOLOCAUST EDUCATION AND MEMORIAL CENTRE OF TORONTO
4600 Bathurst Street
Willowdale, Ontario M2R 3V2
416-635-2883, ext. 144/153
Hours: Tuesday, 1 to 4:30; Thursday, 1 to 4:30, 7 to 9; Sunday, 11 to 4:30. Special arrangements may be made for groups or individuals from out of town.

In an effort to deepen the understanding of the greatest tragedy in recent Jewish history, this memorial center and museum was dedicated in September 1985.

Photographs illustrate themes such as Jewish life in Europe before the war; Jewish social, economic, and political leaders such as Karl Marx, Albert Einstein, and Marc Chagall; and a group specific to this country—the Canadian army liberating the concentration camps.

Display cases hold rescued artifacts such as Torah scrolls, Stars of David, postcards, prison uniforms, calendars, ghetto money, and tea and coffee coupons from Terezin.

Victims of the Holocaust are remembered in the Hall of Memories. Their names are inscribed on ceramic tiles that line the walls. This is a place for meditation and prayer.

One audiovisual presentation explores the roots of anti-Semitism.

Highlight: *On each of the solid bronze doors in the entrance hall is the shape of the Hebrew letter "shin." When both are read together they form the word "shesh," which represents the number 6, in memory of the 6 million people who died in the Holocaust. Behind the letters are flames and clouds. The doors were created by Canadian sculptor Andrew Poza.*

❧ ROM ☞

THE ROYAL ONTARIO MUSEUM
100 Queen's Park
Toronto, Ontario M5S 2C6
416-586-5549
Hours: Wednesday, Friday, Saturday, Sunday, 10 to 6; Tuesday and
Thursday, 10 to 8.

The ROM, as this museum is widely known, is the most important encyclopedic museum of Canada. More than a million people, 30 percent of whom are from outside Canada, visit the ROM every year. When I first visited, I was reminded of the Canadian–British relationship when I saw a mannequin in a mint green satin dress that was worn by Her Majesty Queen Elizabeth II on a visit to Canada in 1957.

The ROM collection spans the arts, archaeology, science, and the decorative arts. "Museum collections exist because people are curious about the material world around them, and want to understand it," a ROM statement succinctly explains. Beyond that truth is another that museum personnel have just begun to discuss among themselves, often in hushed voices. In planning exhibitions, they are, often in ways they themselves fail to recognize, making political statements. What they include or exclude, the slant of the exhibit, and its spin or impact all represent a point of view.

That Canada's major museum has installed a Judaica gallery is more significant and wonderful than it might seem at first glance. Along with the North Carolina Museum of Art and the American Museum of Natural History, the ROM has taken a step toward recognition of the place of Jewish culture in the world. These efforts are to be loudly applauded. Perhaps some other major museums in North America will soon be inclined to follow suit.

The Judaica gallery is one of the nine Samuel European Galleries, which opened in fall of 1989. These galleries are devoted to the decorative arts in Western Europe from the 10th century to the present. The Jewish works, which number more than sixty, date from the 1500s to 1980 and include objects from the Netherlands to Russia. There are two themes: feasts and festivals (Sabbaths, Rosh Hashanah, Yom Kippur, Hanukkah, Purim, and Passover) and the life cycle (birth, marriage, death). These themes, on either side of the gallery, are linked by a display that explores the Torah.

The ROM's Judaica gallery was planned for the purpose of cultural enlightenment rather than to show off the ROM's own collection of artifacts, and many of the objects on display are on loan from other collections. Some important treasures found here are a bonus for visitors. One is a Hanukkah menorah from Venice, dating to the late 1700s.

This Venetian treasure was discovered in the museum's European collection by a student at the University of Toronto, who translated an inscription. The lamp, it was discovered, was made for the Vivante family during a period when the exuberant, lavish, even profligate rococo was waning and there was a move toward simplicity. The brass menorah is simple and elegant in design with gently curving plant motifs and plain, shallow wells for oil. There is nothing ostentatious about it.

In contrast, silver Torah rimmonim from Italy, dated 1811, are elaborate and highly ornamental, in the shape of a crown topped by a pineapple. The base is lacy fretwork with plants and bells incorporated into the design.

One of the most splendid objects is another Italian piece, a cup of Elijah of gilt and white enamel, hand-painted on red glass. I'm inclined to think the scene shows King Solomon, sitting on his throne, because the figure is wearing a crown and he sits on a throne protected by a lion. (According to the bible, lions guarded King Solomon's throne.) This, however, is one of the most human-looking lions one is likely to encounter. It has a person's rather than a feline's nose, and its grimacing expression seems to say "Get me out of here!" Solomon, with his very long white beard, looks quite weary.

Highlight: *This museum is outstanding in many fields. Its Chinese collection is one of the ten most outstanding in the world outside China. There is a Ming Tomb exhibit, showing a tomb built for a general who died in 1654. The massive ornamental gate has marble bas reliefs of dragon-horses. Two giant camels face each other, so stationed as to guard the tomb from invasion by evil spirits. Monumental human figures are there to serve the deceased. The objects are arranged in a traditional "spirit way" configuration, with the altar and tumulus at the end. The effect is powerful. When contrasted to the Judaica exhibit, it provides an educational excursion into comparative religions.*

Silver Torah crown made in Italy in 1811. Courtesy of Royal Ontario Museum, Toronto. (On loan from the Beth Tzedec Reuben and Helene Dennis Museum, Toronto.)

217

This Italian cup of Elijah features gilt and white enamel hand-painted on red glass. Courtesy of Royal Ontario Museum, Toronto. (On loan from the Tzedec Reuben and Helene Dennis Museum, Toronto.)

✌ DISCOVERIES ✌

THE KOFFLER GALLERY
4588 Bathurst Street
North York, Ontario, M2R 1W6
416-636-2145
Hours: Sunday to Thursday, 10 to 4; Tuesday and Wednesday
evenings, 6 to 9; Friday, 9 to noon; closed Saturday and Jewish
holidays.

The Koffler Gallery is devoted to a general cultural enrichment that includes exhibiting, collecting, and documenting all manner of works of contemporary Canadian art. Nevertheless, as part of the gallery's exhibition policy, a large number of exhibitions collect and show Judaica and contemporary Jewish art.

Many important and interesting discoveries remain to be made in the field of Jewish art. An artist whose work came to my attention through the Koffler is Georgia Amar, who was born in Morocco, where the worlds of Judaism, Christianity, and Islam meet. She has explored color in paintings that are stunning in concept and in execution. In *Six Days of Creation*, for instance, we look through six narrow, oblong windows in a thick green wall colored in gradations of green, dark to pale. The landscape beyond is layered of colors from violet to bright gold, and is dominated by an egg-shaped white sun—or moon.

Another of the artists introduced to me through this gallery was given a retrospective at the Koffler in 1989. Aba Bayefsky is one of a small number of Canadian artists whose work was shaped, as the catalog says, "by early experiences of racism, economic depression and war."

Bayefsky was born in a predominantly Jewish neighborhood of Toronto in 1923, the son of a Russian-born linotype operator and a Glasgow-born mother of Russian descent. When they moved out of the area into a gentile enclave, the young boy was taunted and bullied. Although he began painting during a period when the Canadian art scene was dominated by the so-called Group of Seven—artists who painted and celebrated Canadian landscapes—Bayefsky's subjects are very different. Skeletons of concentration camp victims are among them. Much of his work has roughness and an edge of suffering. Some, although not all, is tinted with violence.

Since 1979, a great number of exhibitions have either originated at the Koffler or been brought to the gallery from elsewhere. They have shown traditional Jewish ritual art as well as contemporary works. In 1984, for example, an important collection of Judaica was brought together to illustrate *The Jewish Life Cycle*. As we go to press, preparations are well under way for a juried exhibition called The Jewish Wedding, featuring traditional and contemporary interpretations of the chupa, the ketubah, and the wine goblet.

Highlight: *The Koffler is a branch of the Jewish Community Centre of Toronto. Besides its active exhibitions schedule, it administrates The Koffler Gallery School of Visual Art, for students at all levels and of all ages.*

❧ JEWISH "JUNK" ❧

REUBEN AND HELENE DENNIS MUSEUM
Beth Tzedec
1700 Bathurst Street
Toronto, Ontario M5P 3K3
416-781-3511 or 416-781-5658
Hours: Monday, Wednesday, and Thursday, 11 to 5; Saturday, 12 to 1; Sunday, 10 to 1.

In 1961, a landmark book, *Jewish Art: An Illustrated History* was published. The very concept surprised most people: Jewish art? Weren't the Jews prohibited from creating art by the Second Commandment? As anyone who is holding this text in hand knows, the answer is that Jews have created works of great beauty for their homes and their houses of worship since the beginning of their history. Interpretation of the bible has ranged over the millennia and has permitted, in its most liberal reading, representation of every subject except the Lord. Yet, to this day, a great many people believe there is no such thing as Jewish art.

The groundbreaking work on Jewish art, a complete history tracing the subject back to long before the time of King Solomon, was edited by Cecil Roth, a British historian at Oxford University and editor-in-chief of the *Standard Jewish Encyclopedia*, among other works. In *Commentary* magazine, in 1957, Roth wrote:

I imagine that I must own one of the most preposterous collections of miscellaneous Jewish junk to be found anywhere in the world today in private hands. I have over three hundred manuscripts, dozens of Chanukah lamps, a boxful of ancient coins, a sprinkling of bookplates, scores of illuminated marriage contracts, hundreds of engravings and caricatures, a good amount of domestic and synagogal silver and embroidery, some nice pewter—and just about enough space left over for my wife to squeeze herself into the house when it is absolutely necessary. And I've managed it all on an income which, I must say, is regrettably exiguous.

Today, Roth's collection is at the Beth Tzedec Museum, and junk it's not. It was acquired by the congregation in 1964 when Roth, about to retire from his teaching position at Oxford, was looking for a home for his treasures. The first 800 objects were bought then, and the rest, which he could not part with during his lifetime, were later bought from his widow. Cecil Roth died in 1970.

The most famous object in this collection is a megillah from Kaifeng, China. It calls to mind the mysterious Jewish community that lived in China from the medieval period until its sudden disappearance in the 19th century. The beginning of the megillah scroll, which is dated to the early 19th century and believed to have been accomplished by the last survivors of the lost community, has classical Buddhist and Confucian symbols. At the end of the scroll is an executioner in Chinese dress, and children getting ready for a feast. An illuminated page that has been widely reproduced shows a Chinese man dressed in a golden tunic and wide-legged pants. His feet are pointed in one direction, his torso is twisted, and his head is turned in the opposite direction. It appears as though he is going to shoot an arrow from behind his back. He is framed by Hebrew lettering and lovely motifs including butterflies, dragonflies, flowers, and kites. Because the Hebrew calligraphy is identified as Sephardic in style and the scroll is wound on a roller in the Old World manner, it is believed that this megillah was written by a European, although its illustrator was surely Asian.

Jewish adventurers and merchants traveled through China before the 8th century, when a group of about 1,000 Persian or Indian Jews were welcomed by the emperor in Kaifeng, capital of Hunan Province. Many of these Jews were skilled in dying and printing

Megillah, Kaifeng, China, early 19th century. Illuminated vellum. Courtesy of Beth Tzedec Reuben and Helene Dennis Museum, Toronto, Canada.

222

cotton, and there was, during this period, a chronic silk shortage. The Kaifeng colony was not the only Jewish community of China, but it was the largest. Although these Jews lived in relative religious freedom, they were decimated by a series of natural disasters. Their first synagogue, built in 1153, was rebuilt several times. The last crisis that assaulted them occurred in 1849, when the Yellow River flooded the town. Along with heavy loss of life among the Chinese, hundreds of Jews were killed and their survivors were forced to sell all their possessions and the synagogue.

At the end of World War II, about 250 descendants of the Jews of Kaifeng were identified and the few remaining artifacts, such as Roth's megillah, were acquired from them.

There are about 100 ketubot in this collection. Roth wanted it to be representative of the various regions where Jews settled and to cover different periods of time. The oldest ketubah is from Venice and dates to 5405 (1645). On parchment, the colors of this contract are blue, reds, and gold; the design is detailed with flowers, peacocks, and urns; and the lettering is enframed, in the arched shapes of the decalogue, by tall Corinthian columns elaborately ornamented with gold birds and leafy vines. Barely a centimeter of this ancient piece of parchment is left undecorated. Looking at these ketubot, one cannot help but contemplate the importance and the joyfulness of marriage in the Jewish tradition.

By way of contrast, the collection also includes a very austere piece of paper from Germany, dated 1816. This unusual legal document, called a *get*, is a bill of a divorce.

Hanukkah lamps are of brass, bronze, copper, pewter, and silver and are mainly of the sort meant to be mounted on a wall rather than freestanding. The story of Judith, a popular theme during the Renaissance, is a decorative theme for some of these lamps.

In many Jewish collections we find fancy basins, knives, and pitchers, especially for the rite of circumcision. There are also circumcision chairs. This collection has a rococo, two-seated chair: one of the seats was used by the rabbi and the other was reserved for Elijah, the prophet who ascended to heaven in a chariot of fire. Elijah is a favorite figure in Jewish folklore and religion; a glass of wine is poured for him during Passover seders. Elijah is also invited to the circumcision ceremony, and the seat reserved for him is called Elijah's chair. The chair at Beth Tzedec museum is covered with velvet, and the

Chair of Elijah, wood, carved and giltwood in Louis XV style. Berlin, 1766.
Courtesy of Beth Tzedec Reuben and Helene Dennis Museum, Toronto,
Canada.

frame is gilt wood, gracefully turned and elaborately carved. On the back is a large heraldic emblem, the crowned eagle representing Frederick the Great of Prussia. The chair is dated 1767.

An interesting sidelight of Roth's collection is a selection of anti-Semitic caricatures which, though often painful, reveal the mood of certain times and places. There are also many engravings, portraits, and illustrations of Jewish costumes all over the world, and work by Jewish artists of the 19th and 20th centuries. A spice box fashioned after the city gate of Frankfurt belonged to Nathan Adler, a rabbi and cabalist who lived in the city from 1741 to 1800. A controversial mystic, Adler was excommunicated from time to time, but he founded a yeshiva that became famous.

Highlight: *This collection in Toronto is important not only for its significant items but also in consideration of Cecil Roth, who assembled them — a scholar who devoted some 45 years to thought, writing, acquisition, and celebration of Jewish artistic achievement.*

"Recent investigations and theories have suggested that the place of 'Jewish art' in art history may be far greater than the slender relics would imply when taken in themselves," Cecil Roth wrote in the introduction to his book on Jewish art. "The discovery of the great series of synagogue frescoes at Dura Europos suggests the possibility that Christian ecclesiastical art — on which medieval and eventually modern European art ultimately depend — may have developed out of an anterior synagogal art . . . ."

That is most certainly a thought-provoking if not a revolutionary statement. Dura Europos is dated in the 4th century, and its walls were covered with biblical scenes that are fascinating to scholars of many disciplines. The discovery of Dura Europos makes one wonder how many other such decorated synagogues have vanished. A later synagogue, of the 6th century, was uncovered in 1928 by Israeli farmers while they were digging an irrigation ditch at Beth Alpha. The treasure of this find was a mosaic that is one of the masterpieces of ancient art.

The mosaic took up the entire floor of the synagogue's nave. Walking toward the east wall (facing Jerusalem), past a lion and a ram, the first scene shows the sacrifice of Isaac. Beyond that, in the central area, is a large circle divided into the twelve months, each represented by a sign of the zodiac.

Beth Alpha's mosaic, of stone and colored glass, is both primitive and sophisticated. The people and animals represented have the directness of, for example, medieval and early American art. Yet the composition and colors are elegant and the work is beautiful. Moreover, if there is any vestige of doubt that ancient Jews worked in figurative art, that should be dispelled by both Dura Europos and Beth Alpha.

In the Fellowship Court of Beth Tzedec synagogue is a copy of the central panel of Beth Alpha's mosaic floor, in its original size and color. The replica was made in Israel, with stones of Israel, each chipped by hand. It is an exceptional work in its own right and as a reminder of Jewish history. And it seems appropriate that the place in which the collection of Cecil Roth is housed has a work that serves to remind visitors of some of the earliest examples of Jewish art.

GLOSSARY

ARK   The cabinet in which the Torah is kept.

ASHKENAZI   Jews of Western or Eastern European origin.

B.C.E.   Before the Common Era, an alternative to B.C.

BIMAH   Raised platform in the synagogue, for the reader of the Torah.

CHUPA   A canopy for the wedding ceremony.

DECALOGUE   The Ten Commandments.

ETROG   Citron, a lemon-like fruit.

GROGGER   Rattle used during Purim to obliterate the sound of the name of wicked Haman when the megillah is read.

HAGGADAH (plural: Haggadot)   Liturgy read at seder; the book that contains the liturgy.

HALLAH   Braided bread, made with eggs, used in Sabbath meal ceremony.

HANUKKAH   Commemoration of the rededication of the Temple of Jerusalem in 165 B.C.E., an eight-day festival.

HAVDALAH   Ceremony marking the end of the Sabbath.

HEYMISH   Like home (Yiddish).

KADDISH   Prayer recited by mourners.

KETUBAH (plural: Ketubot)   Marriage contract.

KIDDUSH   The prayer of sanctification said over wine.

LULAV   Palm branch or shoot.

MAHZOR   Book of prayers.

MATZO   Unleavened bread eaten during Passover.

MEGILLAH   A scroll, especially the Book of Esther read on the festival of Purim.

MENORAH   Seven-branched candelabrum.

MEZUZAH (plural: mezuzot)   Hebrew for doorpost; synonymous with the scroll traditionally placed on the right side of a door in a Jewish home.

MIZRACH   East, literally; usually an ornamental design placed on the Eastern wall to show the direction of Jerusalem.

NER TAMID (eternal light)   Small light kept always burning in front of the ark.

PASSOVER (Pesach)   Spring festival commemorating the exodus from Egypt.

PENTATEUCH   First five books of the Bible.

PSALTER   Volume containing the Book of Psalms.

PURIM   Festival commemorating Esther's victory over Haman's attempt to destroy the Jews.

RIMMONIM   Literally, "pomegranates" in Hebrew; the decorative finials that adorn the staves of a Torah scroll.

SEDER   The ritual home service for the first two nights of Passover; includes recitation of the story of the exodus from Egypt.

SEPHARDI (plural: Sephardim)   Jew of Spanish descent.

SHTETL   Small Jewish community in Eastern Europe.

SHOFAR   The ram's horn, blown as a trumpet on special occasions.

SHUL   Synagogue (Yiddish).

SUCCOTH   Festival that recalls the wanderings of the ancient Israelites in the desert.

TALLIS   Prayer shawl.

TEFILLIN (phylacteries)   Small boxes containing biblical passages, bound to left arm and forehead during morning prayer.

TIK   Wood or metal case for Torah scroll.

TORAH   Refers both to the Pentateuch and the entire body of traditional Jewish teaching and literature.

TZEDAKAH   Charity; often refers to a box for alms.

WIMPLE   A Torah binder, usually made from the cloth used to bind a circumcised infant.

ZAMLER   A collector (especially one who collects books for the National Yiddish Book Center).

ZION   At first a hill and fortress in Jerusalem; now refers to Jewish people and their homeland as a symbol of Judaism.

BIBLIOGRAPHY

Freudenheim, T. L. "Books on Art and the Jewish Tradition: 1980–1990," in J. Kabakoff, ed., *Jewish Book Annual*, Vol. 48 (1990–1992). New York: Jewish Book Council, 1991.

Goldstein, D. *Jewish Legends*. New York: P. Bedrick Books, 1987.

Gutmann, J., ed. *Beauty in Holiness: Studies in Jewish Customs and Ceremonial Art*. New York: Ktav, 1970.

Gutmann, J. *Jewish Ceremonial Art*. New York: Thomas Yoseloff, 1964.

The Jewish Museum, New York. *Treasures of the Jewish Museum* (catalog). 1986.

Journal of Jewish Art. Center for Jewish Art, Hebrew University, Jerusalem, Israel.

Kampf, A. *Jewish Experience in the Art of the Twentieth Century*, South Hadley, MA: Bergin and Garvey, 1964.

Kanof, A. *Jewish Ceremonial Art and Religious Observance*. New York: Harry N. Abrams (n. d.).

Kanof, A. *Jewish Symbolic Art*. Jerusalem, Israel: Gefen, 1990.

Narkiss, B., ed. *Picture History of Jewish Civilization*. Israel: L. Amiel, 1978 (available from Chartwell Books, Inc., Secaucus, NJ).

National Museum of American Jewish History, Philadelphia. *The American Jewish Experience* (catalog). 1989.

Roth, C. *Jewish Art: An Illustrated History*. Tel Aviv, Israel: Massadah, 1961.

Schoener, A. *The American Jewish Album: 1654 to the Present*. New York: Rizzoli, 1983.

Weinstein, J. *A Collectors' Guide to Judaica*. London: Thames and Hudson, 1985.

Widoger, G., ed. *Jewish Art and Civilization*. Fribourg, Switzerland: Office du Livre, 1972 (available from Chartwell Books, Inc., Secaucus, NJ).

Index